The Most Basic Japanese

All You Need to Know to Get By

James McGlasson

Aim

This book is meant for those travelling to, moving to or living in Japan, and provides the language basics you will need to get by while there. It aims to give you a grounding in the basic grammar so that you can use the language yourself without the book, as well as use this grammar as a base to learn more. It also gives the phrases for you to get by in several situations that you will naturally find yourself in.

Acknowledgement

A big thanks goes to Hayley Doody (RemoteAssociates.co.uk), who also assisted with constructing this book.

Introduction

To us in the West, Japanese is very exotic and we have the impression that it may be difficult to learn. However, while Japanese has many differences from English, it is relatively easy to learn the rules for basic Japanese, and to begin using the language.

As you will see, sentences in basic Japanese are built with certain rules which, once learned, are simple to follow, making it easy to make basic sentences. In truth, (and although to really become fluent is far from easy) speaking basic Japanese is really not too difficult.

Some of the things that make things simpler for us as learners of basic Japanese, are that the verb forms don't change for each person, there are no articles, pronouns (for basic Japanese) are simple, and the language rules are extremely organized. Also note that Japanese does not have tones, like some other Asian languages.

Japanese becomes more complicated as you learn more, but to begin with, as long as you have the basic grammar rules and language in this book, you will be able to speak quite a lot. As already stated, this book aims to give you exactly what you need to get by – no more, no less.

Also, if you feel this book can be improved in any way for future readers, including any typos and such, I would really appreciate it if you could give me an email to **info@MostBasicLanguages.com** and I will see what I can do – if I do amend anything based on your suggestion, I will send something good in return too. The aim is for this book to be genuinely useful for people, so if you notice anything that you think could or should be changed, then please drop me a line.

How to Use this Book

On arrival and for your first couple of days in Japan, you will need 'The 10 Most Useful Phrases for a Newcomer'.

Then, with just the language in the rest of the book, you can survive in Japan for an extended period of time.

It is advisable to work through the Basic Language section chapter by chapter, and use the Situational Japanese (Phrases) section as and when you find yourself in those situations where you need the phrases and vocab (in a taxi, restaurant, bar and shop).

The chapters are set up so that they can also remain as easy reference tools for you (i.e. so if you have an issue with pronouns in the future, you know exactly where to look, and so on), but this means that some language chapters (e.g. Pronouns & Verbs) contain a lot of information, so what you might want to do, is to take them bit by bit and move on.

For pronouns, a good method could be to learn the Subject, Direct & Indirect Objects to begin with, then move on to verbs (and come back to Possessive later).

For verbs, it would be useful to learn the following verb forms: Present/Future Form & its Negative, Past Form & its Negative, and the Question Form. Then you will have the basics to get by, so can move on to the next chapters, and return later to learn the rest of the verb forms (e.g. 'want to', ordering, 'can' and 'must').

For numbers, you might want to cover just the General section and then the Stating How Many section to begin with, then come back to learn the Higher Numbers and Telling the Time.

It is really up to you, and if you wish to take the basics of these 3 chapters in particular, move on and then come back for more information from them later, then do so. Of course, it is absolutely fine to just work through the chapters from beginning to end too.

The language is presented in both **English** (in **Bold**) and *Japanese* (in *Italics*) with a pronunciation guide [in square brackets].

If you need extra vocab, here is an online Japanese dictionary which gives the words both in Japanese and in our alphabet, so you can still read them without knowing Japanese script: **http://www.docoja.com**.

3

Table of Contents

Extras

1. The 10 Most Useful Phrases for a Newcomer

1. **Hello** – Choose from:

Good morning	*Ohayougozaimasu*	[oh-hah-yoh-goh-zye-mass]
Good afternoon	*Konnichiwa*	[kon-knee-chee-wah]
Good evening	*Konbanwa*	[kon-ban-wah]

(**Goodbye** *Sayounara* [sigh-yoh-nah-rah])

2. **Thank you** *Arigatou* [ah-ree-gah-toh]

(**You're welcome** *Douitashimashite* [doh'ee-tah-shee-mah-sh'teh])

3. **Sorry** *Gomennasa* [goh-men-nah-sigh]

4. **Excuse me** *Sumimasen* [suh-mee-mah-sen]

5. **How much is it?** *Ikura desuka* [ee-kuh-rah dess-kah]

6. **I'd like this, please** *Kore wo kudasai* [koh-reh woh kuh-dah-sigh]
(can be used in a shop)

7. **Please go to…** *...ni itte kudasai* [knee it-teh kuh-dah-sigh]
(in a taxi)

e.g. **Go to the airport** *Kuukou ni itte kudasai*
[kuuh-koh knee it-teh kuh-dah-sigh]

8. **Waiter!** (or: **Excuse me!**) **Check, please!**
Sumimasen! Okaikei wo onegaishimasu!
[suh-mee-mah-sen, oh-kye-kay woh oh-neh-guy-shee-mass]

9. **I don't understand** *Wakarimasen* [wah-kah-ree-mah-sen]

10. **Where is the toilet?** *Toire wa doko desuka*
[toh'ee-reh wah doh-koh dess-kah]

NB: The characters below indicate Male and Female, and are used to identify the men's and women's toilets.

Male 男子 / 殿方 / 紳士

Female 女子 / 婦人

6

BASIC LANGUAGE

2. Pronunciation

Pronunciation in Japanese is fairly easy, when reading the Romanised versions of the language (i.e. in our alphabet), since the words have been transcribed for us to be able to read. When written in our Romanised script, the vowels are the main thing to learn for pronunciation and the consonants are broadly the same as in English, but there are some things to note below. There is also a good Youtube video here, introducing some of the basics of Japanese pronunciation, and is worth watching:
http://www.youtube.com/watch?v=3K3kt_hkvAM.

For this book, we will fairly shortly have available some downloadable podcasts so you can hear the words and sounds as spoken by a native speaker. Please check the website (**www.MostBasicLanguages.com**) to see when it is ready.

A. The pronunciation of the 5 vowels

'a'   Like [ah] in English

'e'   Like [eh] in English

'i'   Like [ee] in English

'o'   Like [oh] in English

'u'   Like [uh] in English

'ou' Like [oh] in English

Dropped Vowels

- In the words or word endings '*desu*' and '*masu*', the final '*u*' has completely dropped from pronunciation, and these are pronounced [dess] and [mass].

- Other vowels that are dropped, are the vowels '*i*' and '*u*' when they come between unvoiced consonants (e.g. ch, h, k, s, sh, t, ts). For example, the verb 'to like' in Japanese is '*suki desu*' – this will be pronounced [ski-dess], with the '*u*' not pronounced.

B. There are a couple of consonants which are pronounced (slightly) differently to in English.

'r'   The [r] is pronounced in the slightly more trilled manner of other European languages, such as French and Spanish.

'd'   Because of the above regarding [r], the [d] is pronounced more strongly than in English, because otherwise it sounds similar to [r].

C. Some sounds we use in English do not exist in Japanese

'l'   There is no [l] sound in Japanese, and any English names including an [l], for example, 'London' will have the [l] replaced with an [r] sound. So this becomes *'Rondon'* [ron-don].

'v'   There is no [v] sound in Japanese, and any English names including a [v], for example, 'Liverpool' will have the [v] replaced with a [b] sound. So this becomes *'Ribapuru'* [ri-bah-poo-ruh].

'f'   There is no [f] sound in Japanese, meaning any [f] sounds in names are pronounced like an [h], for example, 'France' has its [f] replaced by an [h] sound. It becomes *'Huransu'*   [huh-ran-suh].

3. Japanese Sentences

Before we get going with the language, it is useful to know a bit about basic Japanese sentences. Word order can vary in Japanese, but usually, it is a case of **Subject – Object – Verb**. Compare this to English, where we normally see Subject – Verb – Object. Sentences work differently too, so there are a few things we need to learn. So in English, we normally need our subject to come first, followed by the verb, and then followed by the rest of the sentence. We can move things around to form questions and change the emphasis, but note that the order is still important. Compare: "You are going", "Are you going?" and "Going, are you?" In each case, we can clearly see the meaning or emphasis is different.

It doesn't work quite like this in Japanese. For one thing, as stated, the order is normally **Subject – Object – Verb** at its basic level, with the verb coming at the end of the sentence. Where, in English, we work out the sentence meaning (which word is the subject or object, whether it is a question etc) from the word order, Japanese uses little words (called 'particles') to show these same things, so when something is the subject, an added 'particle' tells us this, or when it is the direct or indirect object, different 'particles' are added to show this). This can sometimes make Japanese easier to understand when you are listening, but speaking can be a different matter, because there are so many particles to learn and know when exactly to use them. However, when dealing with basic Japanese, things are easier because we can get by using just a few of these particles (if you continue to learn Japanese, you will learn many more as well as the fine distinctions between some of them).

In fact, what you will find is that, at least for the few particles you will learn in this book, this is something that actually makes basic Japanese quite straightforward to learn. Of course, using a different system of making sentences takes a little getting used to, but as you do become used to it, things become much easier.

So in this chapter, we will describe various grammatical terms in English (subject, direct & indirect objects etc), then outline how to use them in basic Japanese sentences. We are assuming a basic knowledge of the terms noun, verb and adjective. Also note that things (throughout this book) are being labelled as we would in English, although they are not exactly direct equivalents in Japanese. However, for the purposes of this book and quickly getting to grips with the basic language, it is useful to think about them in our terms. If you take Japanese further, you will find many subtle distinctions which are not useful to go into here.

The Particles for Basic Japanese ('wa', 'wo', 'ni' (ind. obj.), 'ni' (location), 'no', 'ka')

Although there are many particles in Japanese, we are going to cover 5 for the purposes of this book. These words come right after the word(s) they refer to. If you want to know more particles, Wikipedia has a very useful reference page for these: **http://en.wikipedia.org/wiki/Japanese_particles**, but to begin with, these 5 will be more than enough to learn.

The 5 particles we will cover for basic Japanese are as follows – you will see them being used in examples throughout the book, so you will have the opportunitiy to see them in use as well:

'wa' [wah]
– This indicates the <u>topic</u> of the sentence (most usually the subject, the person or thing 'doing' the verb).
– 'wa' comes right after the noun it refers to, and in English would mean something like 'As for…' (so something like: "As for Tom, he lives in Tokyo.").
– Although we don't normally state this phrase (as for…) in English, in Japanese, it appears in most sentences to indicate what the topic is.
– For example, 'Watashi wa' ('I', where 'I' is the topic / subject of the sentence, e.g. '**I** want that', really meaning something along the lines of, 'As for me, I want that', although this is not how we would translate it in English).
– The true particle to indicate the subject in Japanese is actually 'ga' (while 'wa'indicates the 'topic'), which you will see in a few places in the book. The reason 'wa' is given here is because the subject is most often the topic, and 'wa' can be used in instances where 'ga' cannot, so 'wa' is more useful and easier to use in basic Japanese.

'wo' [woh]
– This indicates the <u>direct object</u> of the sentence (the person or thing that the verb is 'performed on' or that 'suffers' the verb).
– 'wo' comes right after the direct object to indicate that this is what it is.
– For example, 'Watashi wo' ('me', where 'me' is the direct object of the sentence, e.g. 'He hit **me**').
– Some verbs take 'ga' instead of 'wo' – this will be stated with each relevant verb later.

'ni' (for indirect object)   [knee]

– This indicates the indirect object of the sentence (the person or thing that receives the direct object).

– '*ni*' comes right after either the indirect object.

– For example, "*Watashi ni*" ('to me', where 'me' is the receiver of the direct object, e.g. 'Give it **to me**').

'*ni*' (for location)   [knee]

– This means 'to', 'in', 'at', and is used to show the location where something happens.

– '*ni*' comes right after either the location.

– For location, this is something else that is different to English – where we say, e.g., 'to school' or 'at school', in Japanese, this becomes "*gakkou ni*" ('school at' or 'school in'). This is the case in general for prepositions (to, in, at, on etc) Japanese – where English uses prepositions, Japanese uses 'postpositions', meaning they come after the noun they refer to – the opposite to English.

– As above, "*gakkou ni*" (to/at school).

'*no*'   [noh]

– This indicates the possessive (a person or thing that 'owns' something else).

– '*no*' comes in between the owner and the owned thing (like **apostrophe-S** ('s) does in English).

– For example, '*Watashi no kuruma*' (my car), and '*Tanaka-san no kuruma*' (Mr. Tanaka's car).

'*ka*'   [kah]

– This indicates a question. No question mark is needed in Japanese, because this word tells you it is a question.

– It is really easy to use and is simply added at the very end of the sentence.

– When spoken, it has a rising tone like in English.

– For example,

Your car is red   *Anata no kuruma akai desu*

Is your car red?   *Anata no kuruma akai desu* **ka**

So, to briefly demonstrate again, with some sample sentences, it goes something like this:

She gives it to him > **She** *wa* – **him** *ni* – **it** *wo* – **gives**

Does she give it to him? > **She** *wa* – **him** *ni* – **it** *wo* – **gives** *ka*

12

A Basic Japanese Sentence Structure

As in English, each sentence has a subject and a verb, and maybe direct / indirect objects, as well as others that are unnecessary to cover here. The following is the list of things we need to know to make Japanese sentences, stated in the order in which you can put them in a sentence.

1. Subject – the person or thing that 'does' or 'performs' the verb.
e.g. **I** go to school. **Your friend** wants to come. **She** likes her job. **I** gave the document to him.

2. Question Words – 'what', 'where', 'when', 'who', 'why', 'how'. These are included here because, when used, they come right after the subject / topic in a basic Japanese sentence. Also, when asking questions in Japanese, the word _'ka'_ is added at the end (this is what indicates that it is a question).

3. Receiver or Indirect Object – the person or thing that 'receives' the direct object, so in English, it translates as 'to/for someone or something'. It includes when the sense is that something was given or said to someone (even if the word 'to' or 'for' is not included). ASK YOURSELF: Who or what receives something (the direct object)?
e.g. I gave the document **to him**. I gave **him** the document. He pays **me** my salary.

4. Direct Object – the person or thing that the verb is 'performed on'. ASK YOURSELF: Who or what is the verb performed on? Who or what 'suffers' the verb? (i.e. 'what is given', 'what is wanted', 'what is paid' etc).
e.g. I hit **him**. Your friend wants **a car**. She likes **her job**. I gave **the document** to him. He paid me **my salary**.

5. Extra Information – this can be e.g. adding an adjective or description, or the location, where we use prepositions (in, at, on, to etc) in English. Unlike in English, Japanese prepositions, ('in'/'to' etc) are added after the noun.
e.g. Adding an adjective: My car is **red**. Or adding a location: I drive **to work**. She goes **to school**. The children are **at home**.

6. Verb – action words, 'go', 'do', 'want', 'be/am/is/are'. This is included here since verbs always come last in Japanese sentences.

7. Question Indicator - If it is a question, add the word _'ka'_ at the end of the sentence.

13

- So let's break down a couple of English sentences, and then we'll look at the Japanese equivalents – don't be daunted though – it is a specific set of rules, that you just have to learn once, and they can be learned quite rapidly. Then, you will be able to form Japanese sentences very easily in the future, so take the time to read through this and it will stand you in good stead to learn the rest of the language in this book. Also, this will be explained and shown in examples through the book, so you will be able to get the hang of it as you keep reading.

Example Sentence 1

Let's look at a basic English sentence:
"She gives it to him." or **"She gives him it."**

Subject – who/what is 'doing' the verb?
<u>She</u> gives…
Kanojo wa…

Question Word – 'What?', 'Where?', 'When?', 'Who?', 'Why?', 'How?'
(no question word in this sentence since it is not any kind of question)

Receiver / Indirect Object – who receives the direct object?
She gives it to <u>him</u> / She gives <u>him</u> it
…kare ni…

Direct Object – what does she give?
She gives <u>it</u>…
…sore wo…

Extra information (e.g. location, adjective etc)
(there is no extra information in this sentence)

Verb – what is she doing / does she do?
She <u>gives</u>…
…agemasu

So, in Japanese, this sentence will become:
She – to him – it – gives
Kanojo wa – kare ni – sore wo – agemasu
[kah-noh-joh wah – kah-reh knee – soh-reh woh – ah-geh-mass]

Note the addition of '*wa*', '*ni*' and '*wo*' to indicate subject/topic, indirect object, direct object.

Example Sentence 2

And to look at a second example sentence:
"Does he go to school?"

Subject – who/what is 'doing' the verb?
Does <u>he</u> go…
Kare wa…
('He' is also what is referred to as the 'topic' of this sentence in Japanese – as mentioned, for basic Japanese, this distinction is less important, but you will learn there is a difference if you learn more of the language).

Question Word – 'What?', 'Where?', 'When?', 'Who?', 'Why?', 'How?'
(no question word here – obviously, this is a question, but not using one of the question words)

Receiver / Indirect Object – who receives the direct object?
(no indirect object / receiver in this sentence since no one receives anything)

Direct Object – what does he 'go'?
(no direct object in this sentence – in fact, 'to go' never has a direct object)

Extra Information – Location: where is he 'in / at / on', or where is he going 'to' or 'from'?
Does he go <u>to school</u>?
…gakkou ni…

Verb – what is he doing / does he do? This is a question, so also add '*ka*'.
Does he <u>go</u>…?
…ikimasu + ka

So, in Japanese, this sentence will become:

He – to school – goes?

Kare wa –gakkou ni – ikimasu ka

[kah-reh wah – gak-koh knee – ee-kee-mass kah]

Note the addition of '*wa*', '*ni*' and '*ka*' to indicate subject/topic, location (to school) and question.

If you were to use a question word, you can just insert it after the subject / topic.
e.g. **When?** = *itsu*   [ee-ts'uh]
So we just saw: *Kare wa gakkou ni ikimasuka.*
To insert the question word, 'when', it will simply become:

When does he go to school?   *Kare wa itsu gakkou ni ikimasuka*

SUMMARY

Here are the parts of a basic Japanese sentence:

1. **Subject** (who performs the verb) + *wa*

2. **Question Word** (see Questions chapter)

3. **Receiver / Indirect Object** (receives the direct object) + *ni*

4. **Direct Object** (who/what the verb is performed on) + *wo*

5. **Any Extra Information**
- **Location** (where it happens) + *ni*
- **Adjective** (description)

6. **Verb** (with relevant ending)

16

4. Pronouns

I/me, you, he/she, we/us, they/them, my/mine, your/yours etc.

We can get by in basic Japanese by learning 7 pronouns plus 4 particles (3 we have already seen) that are added after the pronouns, making things slightly easier to learn (at least in this respect) than for people learning English.

So here, we will cover these 7 words (I, you, he, she, we, you, they), and then the various particles which are added – remember, these words indicate whether it is the subject (I, we) or object (me, us) of the sentence, or used as a possessive (my, our). In fact, there are more pronouns and more complicated rules surrounding their use, but again, in the beginning, and since we are learning what we need to get by, these are things that can be learned later.

So first, let's see the basic Japanese pronouns. These are the base words, that are used in Japanese no matter what case – subject (I, she), direct object (me, her), indirect object (to me, to her) or possessive (my, mine, her, hers), which makes our initial job as learners a bit easier.

One thing to note, is that it is natural in Japanese to speak somewhat 'impersonally', so pronouns will very often be dropped. In the beginning, this can seem confusing when you hear it, but you will begin to get used to it as you communicate more in the language.

Singular

I, me, etc	*Watashi*	[wah-tah-shee]
You (sg.)	*Anata*	[ah-nah-tah]
He	*Kare*	[kah-reh]
She	*Kanojo*	[kah-noh-joh]

Plural   ('*tachi*' indicates the plural)

We	*Watashitachi*	[wah-tah-sh'tah-chee]
You (pl.)	*Anatatachi*	[ah-nah-tah tah-chee]
They	*Karera*	[kah-reh-rah]

And now let's look at how these words are used in practice, using the additional 4 particle that were mentioned above. You will see below that this is actually pretty simple.

Subject Pronouns (I, he, we etc): '... wa' [wah]

Subject pronouns are used in a similar way to English, and they come at the beginning of a sentence. For these, we take the words from the list above, and add the particle *'wa'* [wah] to indicate that it is the subject (really, the topic, as previously stated). So we can consider the subject pronouns as follows:

I	*Watashi wa*
You (sg.)	*Anata wa*
He	*Kare wa*
She	*Kanojo wa*
We	*Watashitachi wa*
You (pl.)	*Anatatachi wa*
They	*Karera wa*

Examples:

I am English
Watashi wa Igirisu-jin desu
[wah-tah-shee wah ee-ghee-ree-suh-jin dess]

You are Japanese
Anata wa Nihon-jin desu
[ah-nah-tah wah knee-hon-jin dess]

She is American
Kanojo wa Amerika-jin desu
[kah-noh-joh wah ah-meh-ree-kah-jin dess]

We live in Tokyo
Watashitachi wa Tokyo ni sunde imasu
[wah-tah-sh'tah-chee wah Tokyo knee suh'n-deh ee-mass]

Direct Object Pronouns (me, him, us etc): '... wo' [woh]

The word added to indicate direct object pronouns is 'wo' [woh] (again, there are other words that also indicate this, with subtle nuances, but to get by in the beginning, this one will suffice).

In English, the direct object comes after the verb, so we say, for example: "I see him". But in Japanese, the object comes before the verb (the verb is the last word in a Japanese sentence) so, in Japanese, you would say: "I him see" instead. There is more information on this in the Japanese Sentences chapter.

Me	Watashi wo
You	Anata wo
Him	Kare wo
Her	Kanojo wo
Us	Watashitachi wo
You	Anatatachi wo
Them	Karera wo

Examples:

She sees me (becomes "She me sees")
Kanojo wa watashi wo miteimasu
[kah-noh-joh wah wah-tah-shee woh mee-tay-mass]

He loves her (becomes "He her loves")
Kare wa kanojo wo aishiteimasu
[kah-reh wah kah-noh-joh woh eye-sh'tay-mass]

They help us (becomes "They us help")
Karera wa watashitachi wo tasukete kuremasu
[kah-reh-rah wah wah-tah-sh'tah-chee woh tah-s'keh-teh kuh-reh-mass]

Indirect Object Pronouns (to me, to him, to us etc): '... ni' [knee]

We've already seen that '*ni*' [knee] indicates the person or thing that receives the direct object, and the English equivalent for this is 'to me' or 'for me'. E.g. "He gives the book to me", where it is 'me' who receives 'the book'.

So here, the word '*ni*' is added after the pronoun, and you will see in the examples how this replaces 'to me' etc.

Also re-visit the Japanese Sentences chapter if you need to, because this is where it can seem a little complicated. This one normally comes after the subject, and before the direct object, and the verb comes at the very end - although this is confusing in the beginning, once you learn it, it all becomes quite straightforward because you can use the same structure every each time.

To me	*Watashi ni*
To you	*Anata ni*
To him	*Kare ni*
To her	*Kanojo ni*
To us	*Watashitachi ni*
To you	*Anatatachi ni*
To them	*Karera ni*

Examples

I give it to him. Or: **I give him it** (becomes "I to him it give")
Watashi wa kare ni sore wo agemasu
[wah-tah-shee wah kah-reh knee soh-reh woh ah-geh-mass]

She gives it to me. Or: **She gives me it** (becomes "She to me it gives")
Kanojo wa watashi ni sore wo kuremasu
[kah-noh-joh wah wah-tah-shee knee soh-reh woh kuh-reh-mass]

They give it to you. Or: **They give you it** (becomes "They to you it give")
Karera wa anata ni sore wo agemasu
[kah-reh-rah wah ah-nah-tah knee soh-reh woh ah-geh-mass]

Possessive

The next thing to know about pronouns is how to show possession. As in English, there are 2 ways to show possession ('my'/'your'/'her' etc, and 'mine'/'yours'/'hers' etc):

1. My, Your, Our etc
'**My car**' - the word to add for this is '*no*' [noh] – therefore: 'pronoun + *no* + noun' = Eng. 'my + noun'

My	*Watashi no*
Your (sg.)	*Anata no*
His	*Kare no*
Her	*Kanojo no*
Our	*Watashitachi no*
Your (pl.)	*Anatatachi no*
Their	*Karera no*

So, for this one (**my car**), we just need to say the 'pronoun + *no* + noun' which, in this case, is '**I** + *no* + **car**' (car = *kuruma* [kuh-ruh-mah]). Therefore:

***Watashi no** kuruma...* = My car...
***Kanojo no** tokei...* = Her watch...

And this will be followed by the particles we have seen before ('*wa*', '*wo*', '*ni*' etc) as necessary.

e.g. ***Watashi no kuruma wa** akairo desu* = My car is red.
(**My car** *wa* (for subj.) + **red** + **is**)

2. Mine, Yours, Ours etc
' The/that car is **mine**' - here, the words added are '*no mono*' [noh moh-noh] – so, 'pronoun + *no mono* + is' (...**is** mine). We also need to indicate that the noun is the subject in this sentence (as seen before, by adding '*wa*' after the noun).

Mine	*Watashi no mono*
Yours (sg.)	*Anata no mono*
His	*Kare no mono*
Hers	*Kanojo no mono*
Ours	*Watashitachi no mono*
Yours (pl.)	*Anatatachi no mono*
Theirs	*Karera no mono*

So, for this one (**is mine**), we need to say the 'noun + *wa*, + pronoun + *no mono* + is. So, in this case, '**That car** *wa* + **I** *no mono* + **is**'.

21

Sono kuruma wa **watashi no mono** *desu* = The car is mine.
Sono kuruma wa **kanojo no mono** *desu* = The car is hers.

Examples:

He is <u>our friend</u> (becomes "He <u>our</u> friend is")
Kare wa <u>watashitachi no tomodachi</u> desu
[kah-reh wah wah-tah-sh'tah-chee noh toh-moh-dah-chee dess]

<u>Her</u> son is at school (becomes "<u>Her</u> son at school is")
<u>Kanojo no musuko</u> wa gakkou ni imasu
[kah-noh-joh noh muh-s'koh gak-koh knee ee-mass]

<u>My</u> car is red (becomes "<u>My</u> car red is")
<u>Watashi no kuruma</u> wa akairo desu
[wah-tah-shee noh kuh-ruh-mah wah ah-kye-roh dess]

The red car is <u>mine</u> (becomes "The red car <u>mine</u> is")
Sono akai kuruma wa <u>watashi no mono</u> desu
[soh-noh ah-kye kuh-ruh-mah wah wah-tah-shee-noh-moh-noh dess]

SUMMARY

<u>Singular:</u> *Watashi, Anata, Kare, Kanojo*

<u>Plural:</u> *Watashitachi, Anatatachi, Karera*

<u>Subject</u> (I, he, we): + *wa*

<u>Direct object</u> (me, him, us): + *wo*

<u>Indirect object</u> (to/for me / him / us): + *ni*

<u>Possessive</u> (my, his, our): + *no* + noun; (mine, ours): + *no mono* + is

22

5. The Verb 'to be'

This is included here in its own chapter, because there are some important differences between Japanese and English. Where we just have one verb 'to be' in English, in Japanese there are 3 words to learn, which are used in different situations.

Desu

This is used when 'to be' really means something 'equates to' something else ('something = something'). What this means is that when you are saying things like "The car is red", "I am a student", "We are English" or "He is 30", then we use '*desu*', pronounced [dess].

I'm a student
Watashi wa gakusei desu   [wah-tah-shee wah gah-k'say dess]

She is Japanese
Kanojo wa nihonjin desu   [kah-noh-joh wah knee-hon-jin dess]

He is 30 years old
Kare wa sanjussai desu   [kah-reh wah san-juh-sigh dess]

Imasu & Arimasu

These two are somewhat similar, and carry the sense of 'exist', and are used to mean 'there is/are'.

'*Imasu*' is used when referring to any living thing (including people, animals and even insects), while '*arimasu*' is used when talking about inanimate objects.

There are 3 people (in the classroom)
(Kyoushitsu niwa) **san nin imasu**
[k'yoh-sh-ts'uh knee-wah san nin ee-mass]

There are lots of animals (in the zoo)
(Doubutsuen niwa) doubutsu ga **takusan imasu**
[doh-buh-ts'uh-en knee-wah doh-buh-ts'uh gah tah-k'san ee-mass]

There is one chair
Isu ga **hitotsu arimasu**   [ee-suh gah h'toh-ts'uh]

23

Note that when saying 'there is/are', '*ga*' is normally used instead of '*wa*' – so the basic construction for 'there is' / 'there are' is: Noun + *ga* – (number if required) – *imasu / arimasu* (for living / non-living things).

Easy Practice

Cover the answers on the next page and select the correct verb (*desu, imasu* or *arimasu*) for each of these sentences. Then look over the page to check your answers. Remember the verb comes at the end:

1. **There is a television** (*terebi*): "**Television** *ga* <u>**there is**</u>"

2. **The television is big** (*ookii*):
"**Television** *wa* **big** <u>**is**</u>"

3. **There is a cat** (*neko*):
"**Cat** *ga* <u>**there is**</u>"

4. **The cat is small** (*chiisai*):
"**Cat** *wa* **small** <u>**is**</u>"

5. **There are many** (*takusan*) **cats** (*neko*):
"**Cats** *ga* **many** <u>**there are**</u>"

Easy Practice Answers

There is a television
Terebi ga arimasu   [teh-reh-bee gah ah-ree-mass]

The television is big
Terebi wa ookii desu   [teh-reh-bee wah oh-kee dess]

There is a cat
Neko ga imasu   [neh-koh gah ee-mass]

The cat is small
Neko wa chiisai desu   [neh-koh wah chee-sigh dess]

There are many cats
Neko ga takusan imasu   [neh-koh gah tah-k'san ee-mass]

6. Verbs

6a. General

Japanese verbs work completely differently to English verbs, and although it might take a little bit of time getting used to them, overall, they are easier to learn and use than English or most European languages.

The main things we need to know about verbs in Japanese are as follows:

- Verbs always come at the very end of a sentence (as discussed in the Sentences chapter)

- There are 2 main groups of Japanese verbs, which have different endings.

- There are a couple of common irregular verbs, which do not fit into the 2 groups.

- Generally, there are 2 forms for each tense, one for more formal situations and one for informal - in this book, we will cover the more formal one and ignore the informal one, because you will most likely be speaking to people you do not know, at least in the beginning. After you have the language in this book, you can learn the less formal forms later on.

- Verbs do not change their form or endings for each person (like they do in most European languages)

- Verbs do, however, change their endings to change the meaning of the verb
  a) This includes obvious changes like for the present/future tenses (do / will do), the past (did), negatives (don't / didn't) - just like we change the verb for these in English.
  b) More interestingly, this also includes changes where we would add another verb in English, e.g. must, can, want – where in English, we add these modal verbs to change the meaning, in Japanese, the verb ending changes instead.

While the above sounds complicated, bear in mind this is a very quick summary of the main rules surrounding Japanese verbs - so have a second read the above list to get your head around it a bit, and then move onto the actual mechanics coming up next. Also bear in mind that, although some of it might sound difficult, like the verbs changing their endings for 'can', 'must' etc, it is actually quite simple because there is only one ending for each different meaning – no changes for I, you, he / she etc. The slight problem this can cause when you are starting out, is when Japanese people drop the pronouns, and you have to guess who is acting from the context.

6b. Verb Groups

Each verb form is made by taking the <u>verb stem</u> and then adding the <u>verb ending</u>. There are 3 groups of verbs, all of which generally take the same endings, but what changes is how the stem is formed from the main form of the verb. There are several forms of the verb, but the main 'dictionary form' of the verb ends in '-*u*'.

All the verbs given below are in the format:
Engl. infinitve   *Jp. main form*   (*Jp. verb stem*)   *Jp. polite present tense*

This format enables you to see how the stem is formed for each group, as well as how to form the polite present tense (simply by adding the ending '-*masu*' onto the verb stem).

Group 1
The first verb group in Japanese is verbs that change the final '-*u*' to an '-*i*' to form the stem. Some verbs in group 1 are below. Each is given in its main form, and then the stem in brackets / parentheses (remember, the other verb forms will be various endings attached to this stem).

Some Group 1 Verbs

to buy
kau   (*kai-*)   *kaimasu*   [kye-mass]

to drink
nomu   (*nomi-*)   *nomimasu*   [noh-mee-mass]

to go
iku   (*iki-*)   *ikimasu*   [ee-kee-mass]

to know
shiru   (*shiri-*)   *shirimasu*   [shee-ree-mass]

to listen
kiku   (*kiki-*)   *kikimasu*   [k'kee-mass]

to need
iru   (*iri-*)   *irimasu*   [ee-ree-mass]

to read
yomu   (*yomi-*)   *yomimasu*   [yoh-mee-mass]

to speak
hanasu   (*hanashi-*)   *hanashimasu*   [hah-nah-shee-mass]

27

to understand
wakaru   (*wakari-*)   *wakarimasu*   [wah-kah-ree-mass]

to wait
matsu   (*matsi-*)   *matsimasu*   [mah-ts'ee-mass]

to write
kaku   (*kaki-*)   *kakimasu*   [kah-kee-mass]

Group 2

The second verb groups contains verbs that end in '*-ru*' ('*-iru*' or '*-eru*') and change these endings to '*-i*' when changing their forms. But note that while all verbs in Group 2 end in '*-iru*' or '*-eru*', this does not mean that all verbs ending in these are in Group 2 (for example, *shiru* – to know & *iru* – to need, are in Group 1).

Verbs ending in '*-iru*'

to believe
shinjiru   (*shinji-*)   *shinjimasu*   [shin-jee-mass]

to get off
oriru   (*ori-*)   *orimasu*   [oh-ree-mass]

to get up
okiru   (*oki-*)   *okimasu*   [oh-kee-mass]

to see
miru   (*mi-*)   *mimasu*   [mee-mass]

to wear
kiru   (*ki-*)   *kimasu*   [kee-mass]

Verbs ending in '*-eru*'

to eat
taberu   (*tabe-*)   *tabemasu*   [tah-beh-mass]

to give
ageru   (*age-*)   *agemasu*   [ah-geh-mass]

to go out
deru   (*de-*)   *demasu*   [deh-mass]

to open
akeru   (*ake-*)   *akemasu*   [ah-keh-mass]

to sleep
neru   (*ne-*)   *nemasu*   [neh-mass]

Group 3
The third verb group contains just two verbs, which are irregular. The verbs are:

to come
kuru   (*ki-*)   *kimasu*   [kee-mass]

to do
suru   (*shi-*)   *shimasu*   [shee-mass]

6c Verb Forms

As already stated, all the verb forms given in this chapter are the normal polite forms, as this is the level of Japanese you will need to speak in most instances when visiting the country.

You will see that Japanese verb forms are actually very easy to learn and use for a couple of reasons.

The verb forms are easy to know and use
It is just a case of adding the ending to the verb stem. Verb stem + Verb ending.
e.g. 'to go': *iki + masu*

The verb endings don't change for each person
So, for example, the present / future ending is '-*masu*', and this goes for every verb and every person. So, for example, to say 'I eat', the verb is '*tabemasu*', and this stays the same for 'you / he / she / we / they eat(s)'. Similarly, 'I / you / he / she / we / you / they drink' is '*nomimasu*'.

You don't need to know extra words to add to verbs
In English, we need to learn many words, constructions and changes in word order to use verbs properly, but in Japanese, all of this can be covered by just changing the verb ending. If you compare the example sentences, you will see that the sentences can be exactly the same, with the only change being the verb ending. (e.g. 'She goes to school' – '*Kanojo wa gakkou ni ikimasu*'. 'She doesn't go to school' – *Kanojo wa gakkou ni ikimasen*', 'Does she go to school?' – *Kanojo wa gakkou ni ikimasuka*).

This makes things easy when you are speaking because you just need to change the verb ending (and the rest of the sentence is easy), but means you should pay attention when listening because, unlike in English, you won't know whether the sentence is e.g. present, past, statement, question, positive or negative until you hear the very last word. Obviously, this is another thing you just need to get used to, and you will do as you practise speaking the language.

What this section will cover
In this chapter, we will go through the most important verb forms one by one, and then there will be a summary at the end. This way, you can learn each one as you go, and then have a list where it will be easy to find what you need in the future.

The verb forms necessary for speaking basic Japanese, which are given in this chapter are (see over the page):

1. Present / Future Tense (go, will go):

Where we have both present and future tenses, Japanese has just one, considered as the "incomplete" tense, meaning actions have not been completed (as opposed to the "complete" tense, or what we can call the past tense).

Verb Ending: '-masu' [-mass]

So we just need to add the ending '-masu' onto the verb stem. Let's look at some examples.

To Go (Stem: *iki-*)
Go, goes, will go *ikimasu* [ee-kee-mass]

I go to school
Watashi wa gakkou ni ikimasu
[wah-tah-shee wah gak-koh knee ee-kee-mass]

You will go to school
Anata wa gakkou ni ikimasu
[ah-nah-tah wah gak-koh knee ee-kee-mass]

Notice that the verb form remains the same, whether for 'I', 'you' etc.

To Give (Stem: *age-*)
Give, gives, will give *agemasu* [ah-geh-mass]

She gives it to him
Kanojo wa kare ni sore wo agemasu
[kah-noh-joh wah kah-reh knee soh-reh woh ah-geh-mass]

They will give her a car
Karera wa kanojo ni kuruma wo agemasu
[kah-reh-rah wah kah-noh-joh knee kuh-ruh-mah wo ah-geh-mass]

2. Negative of the Present / Future (don't go, won't go):

Verb Ending: '-masen' [-mah-sen]

So, exactly the same as before, we just need to add the ending '-masen' onto the verb stem. If you compare these examples to the one above (in no.1), you will see that the sentences are exactly the same, with the only change being the verb ending.

To Go (Stem: *iki-*)
Don't / doesn't / won't go   *ikimasen*   [ee-kee-mah-sen]

I don't go to school   *Watashi wa gakkou ni ikimasen*
[wah-tah-shee wah gak-koh knee ee-kee-mah-sen]

You won't go to school   *Anata wa gakkou ni ikimasen*
[ah-nah-tah wah gak-koh knee ee-kee-mah-sen]

Notice again that the verb form remains the same.

To Give (Stem: *age-*)
Don't / doesn't / won't give   *agemasen*   [ah-geh-mah-sen]

She doesn't give it to him
Kanojo wa kare ni sore wo agemasen
[kah-noh-joh wah kah-reh knee soh-reh woh ah-geh-mah-sen]

They won't give her a car
Karera wa kanojo ni kuruma wo agemasen
[kah-reh-rah wah kah-noh-joh knee kuh-ruh-mah woh ah-geh-mah-sen]

3. Past Tense (went):

You will remember that the present / future tense was referred to above as the "incomplete" tense. The past tense in Japanese is really thought of as the **"complete" tense**, in that it refers to actions that have been completed.

Verb Ending: '-mashita'   [-mah-sh'tah]

It should be becoming clear now, that all this means is adding the ending '-mashita' onto the verb stem, so let's see it with the same examples as before.

To Go (Stem: iki-)
Went   ikimashita   [ee-kee-mah-sh'tah]

I went to school
Watashi wa gakkou ni ikimashita
[wah-tah-shee wah gak-koh knee ee-kee-mah-sh'tah]

You went to school
Anata wa gakkou ni ikimashita
[ah-nah-tah wah gak-koh knee ee-kee-mah-sh'tah]

As before, notice that the verb form remains the same.

To Give (Stem: age-)
Gave   agemashita   [ah-geh-mah-sh'tah]

She gave it to him
Kanojo wa kare ni sore wo agemashita
[kah-noh-joh wah kah-reh knee soh-reh woh ah-geh-mah-sh'tah]

They gave her a car
Karera wa kanojo ni kuruma wo agemashita
[kah-reh-rah wah kah-noh-joh knee kuh-ruh-mah woh ah-geh-mah-sh'tah]

4. Negative of the Past (didn't go):

Verb Ending: '-masendeshita'   [-mah-sen deh-sh'tah]

Just as with the endings before, we now just add the ending '-masendeshita' onto the verb stem. Again, the examples given are the same sentences as above – just the verb form is changing.

To Go (Stem: iki-)

Didn't go   *ikimasen deshita*   [ee-kee-mah-sen deh-sh'tah]

I didn't go to school
Watashi wa gakkou ni ikimasen deshita
[wah-tah-shee wah gak-koh knee ee-kee-mah-sen deh-sh'tah]

You didn't go to school
Anata wa gakkou ni ikimasen deshita
[ah-nah-tah wah gak-koh knee ee-kee-mah-sen deh-sh'tah]

To Give (Stem: *age-*)
Didn't give   *agemasen deshita*   [ah-geh-mah-sen deh-sh'tah]

She didn't give it to him
Kanojo wa kare ni sore wo agemasen deshita
[kah-noh-joh wah kah-reh knee soh-reh woh ah-geh-mah-sen deh-sh'tah]

They didn't give her a car
Karera wa kanojo ni kuruma wo agemasen deshita
[kah-reh-rah wah kah-noh-joh knee kuh-ruh-mah woh ah-geh-mah-sen deh-sh'tah]

5. Questions (do / will you go?):

Making questions in Japanese is just a case of adding '-ka' onto the end of the relevant form of the verb.

Verb Ending (for present / future tense): '-masuka'   [-mass-kah]

You will notice that for the present / future tense, both '-masu' and '-ka' are being added, to make the ending '-masuka'.

To Go (Stem: *iki-*)
Do / will you go?　　*ikimasuka*　　　[ee-kee-mass-kah]

Does he go to school?
Kare wa gakkou ni ikimasuka
[kah-reh wah gak-koh knee ee-kee-mass-kah]

Will you go to school
Anata wa gakkou ni ikimasuka
[ah-nah-tah wah gak-koh knee ee-kee-mass-kah]

To Give (Stem: *age-*)
Do / will you give?　　*agemasuka*　　[ah-geh-mass-kah]

Will she give it to him?
Kanojo wa kare ni sore wo agemasuka
[kah-noh-joh wah kah-reh knee soh-reh woh ah-geh-mass-kah]

Will they give her a car?
Karera wa kanojo ni kuruma wo agemasuka
[kah-reh-rah wah kah-noh-joh knee kuh-ruh-mah woh ah-geh-mass-kah]

Also note that you can add '*ka*' onto the end of the other verb forms too, to turn them into questions.
e.g. **Did you go to school?** – *Anata wa gakkou ni ikimashita ka*

If this is your first time going through the book, this is the point you might want to move onto the next section, which shows a list of common verbs (skipping the remaining Verb Forms for the moment, and you can come back to them later).

So, if you would like to skip the other Verb Forms for now, feel free to head to the next chapter, or turn the page to continue on and see them.

6. Want (want to go):

To indicate this in Japanese, the verb form is changed, just like in the cases above.

Verb Ending: '-tai desu'   [-tie dess]

To Go (Stem: *iki-*)
Want to go   *ikitai desu*   [ee-kee-tie dess]

I want to go to school
Watashi wa gakkou ni ikitai desu
[wah-tah-shee wah gak-koh knee ee-kee-tie dess]

To Give (Stem: *age-*)
Want to give   *agetai desu*   [ah-geh-tie dess]

She wants to give it to him
Kanojo wa kare ni sore wo agetai desu
[kah-noh-joh wah kah-reh knee soh-reh woh ah-geh-tie dess]

They want to give her a car
Karera wa kanojo ni kuruma wo agetai desu
[kah-reh-rah wah kah-noh-joh knee kuh-ruh-mah woh ah-geh-tie dess]

7. Politely Ordering (to service staff, taxi drivers etc):

The form of the verb used for this is called the '-*te*' form of the verb, and 'please'
(*kudasai*) is added to it for a polite request.

Verb Form: The '*te*' form of the verb + 'please'
Verb Ending: '-*te kudasai*'   [-teh kuh-dah-sigh]

To Go (Stem: *it-*)
Please go   *itte kudasai*   [it-teh kuh-dah-sigh]
Please go to school *Gakkou ni itte kudasai*   [gak-koh knee it-teh kuh-dah-sigh]

To Eat (Stem: *tabe-*)
Please eat   *tabete kudasai*   [tah-beh-teh kuh-dah-sigh]

To Come (Stem: *ki-*)
Please come   *Kite kudasai*   [k'teh kuh-dah-sigh]
Please come here *Koko ni kite kudasai*   [koh-koh knee k'teh kuh-dah-sigh]

8. Can, to be able to (can go):

Where we add the verb 'can' in English, this is yet another case in Japanese where the same meaning is expressed simply by changing the verb form itself.

What is different here, is that it is not just the ending but the stem that changes. So, the ending remains '-masu' for the present tense, but the stem that is used is different. For this, we need to go back and take the main verb form (e.g. 'iku' for 'to go' or 'ageru' for 'to give'), and to replace the final '-u' with '-e', then add the ending '-masu'.

Verb Stem: Main form of the verb, changing final '-u' to '-e'
Verb Ending: '-masu'   [-mass]

To Go ('iku', so we use 'ike-')
Can go　　　　*ikemasu*　　　　　[ee-keh-mass]

I can go to school
Watashi wa gakkou ni ikemasu
[wah-tah-shee wah gak-koh knee ee-keh-mass]

You can go to school?
Anata wa gakkou ni ikemasu
[ah-nah-tah wah gak-koh knee ee-keh-mass]

To Give (Main verb form: *ageru*, so we use '*agere-*')
Can give　　　　*ageremasu*　　　　[ah-geh-reh-mass]

She can give it to him
Kanojo wa kare ni sore wo ageremasu
[kah-noh-joh wah kah-reh knee soh-reh woh ah-geh-reh-mass]

They can give her a car
Karera wa kanojo ni kuruma wo ageremasu
[kah-reh-rah wah kah-noh-joh knee kuh-ruh-mah woh ah-geh-reh-mass]

9. Must, to have to (must go, have to go):

As with 'can', 'must' is another situation where the verb form is changed to indicate the meaning. Also, like with 'can', it is not just the ending that changes, but the verb stem used is different here too. In fact, it is the main verb form (with no change) that just becomes the verb stem.

Verb Stem: Main verb form
Verb Ending: '-bekidesu'   [-beh-kee-dess]

To Go (Main verb form: *iku-*)
Must go   *ikubekidesu*   [ee-kuh-beh-kee-dess]

He must go to school
Kare wa gakkou ni ikubekidesu
[kah-reh wah gak-koh knee ee-kuh-beh-kee-dess]

You must go to school
Anata wa gakkou ni ikubekidesu
[ah-nah-tah wah gak-koh knee ee-kuh-beh-kee-dess]

To Give (Main verb form: *ageru*)
Must give   *agerubekidesu*   [ah-geh-ruh-beh-kee-dess]

She must give it to him
Kanojo wa kare ni sore wo agerubekidesu
[kah-noh-joh wah kah-reh knee soh-reh woh ah-geh-ruh-beh-kee-dess]

They must give her a car
Karera wa kanojo ni kuruma wo agerubekidesu
[kah-reh-rah wah kah-noh-joh knee kuh-ruh-mah woh ah-geh-ruh-beh-kee-dess]

SUMMARY

Present / Future Tense: Stem + *-masu*

Present / Future Negative: Stem + *-masen*

Past Tense: Stem + *-mashita*

Past Negative: Stem + *-masen deshita*

Questions: Any form + *-ka*

Want to: Stem + *-tai desu*

Polite Ordering: 'Te' form + *kudasai*

Can: Main Verb (change '-u' to '-e') + *-masu* / *-masen*

Must: Main Verb + *-bekidesu*

6d. Some Common Verbs

Note that in the following list of verbs, they are given in this format: *Main form – Verb Stem – Polite Form (present/future tense) – Group – 'Te' Form (to give orders)*. Remember that you will be using the polite form, so this is the form given in the examples below.

Be/am/is/are:

1. ~ a 'state' or 'is equal to'
desu
  e.g. *Watashi wa sensei / gakusei desu* – I am a teacher / student

2. ~ exists
iru (living things)   (*i-*)   *imasu*   (Group 1)
aru (inanimate objects)   (*ari-*)   *arimasu*   (Group 1)

If you need to recap, see the **'To be'** chapter.

Believe
shinjiru (*shinji-*)   *shinjimasu*   (Group 2)   ('te' form: *shinjite*)
  e.g. *Anata wa watashi wo shinjimasuka* – Do you believe me?

Bring
motte kuru (*motte ki-*)   *motte kimasu*   (Group 3, from '*kuru*')
('te' form: *motte kite*)
  e.g. *Biiru wo ni-hon motte kite kudasai* – Bring 2 bottles of beer, please

Buy
kau   (*kai-*)   *kaimasu*   (Group 1)   ('te' form: *katte*)
  e.g. *Watashi wa kuruma wo kaitai desu* – I want to buy a car

Can / be able to:

1. 'Can do' (with the verb '*suru*', 'to do', including with verbs using '*suru*', e.g. '*unten suru*' (drive) & '*ryokou suru*' (travel)).
deku (*deki*)   *dekimasu*
  e.g. *Watashi wa sore wo dekimasu* – I can do it.
  e.g. *Karera wa unten dekimasen* – They can't drive.

2. 'Can' with other verbs, this can be formed by changing the verb ending (-*emasu/-emasen*). See 'Can' in the Verb Forms section.
  e.g. *Kanojo wa oyogemasuka* – Can she swim?

Come

kuru (*ki-*) *kimasu* (Group 3) ('te' form: *kite*)
  e.g. *Kare wa kimasen* – He isn't coming
  e.g. *Koko ni kite kudasai* – Come here, please

Come back

Modoru (*modori-*) *modorimasu* (Group 1) ·('te' form: *modotte*)
  e.g. *Karera wa modorimasu* – They're coming back

Do

suru (*shi-*) *shimasu* (Group 3) ('te' form: *shite*)
  e.g. *Shukudai wo shimashita ka* – Did you do your homework?

Drink

nomu (*nomi-*) *nomimasu* (Group 1) ('te' form: *nonde*)
  e.g. *Anata wa osake wo nomimasuka* – Do you drink rice wine?
  e.g. *Anata wa nani wo nomitai desuka* – What do you want to drink?

Drive

unten suru (*unten shi-*) (Group 3) ('te' form: *unten shite*)
  e.g. *Kare wa nichiyoubi ni kuruma wo unten shimasu* – He drives a car every Sunday

Eat

taberu (*tabe-*) *tabemasu* (Group 2) ('te' form: *tabete*)
  e.g. *Watashi wa niku wo tabemasen* – I don't eat meat

Give (to me, the speaker)

kureru (*kure-*) (Group 2) ('te' form: *kurete*)
  e.g. *Kare wa watashi ni kore wo kuremashita* – He gave me this
(Note: To request something, e.g. "Give me that", it is better and more polite to say 'please' in place of the verb: *Sore wo (watashi ni) kudasai*).

Give (not to me, the speaker)

ageru (*age-*) *agemasu* (Group 2) ('te' form: *agete*)
  e.g. *Kanojo wa kare ni sore wo agemashita* – She gave him that

Go

iku (*iki-*) *ikimasu* (Group 1) ('te' form: *itte*)
  e.g. *Kuukou ni itte kudasai* – Please go to the airport (can be used in a taxi)
  e.g. *Watashi wa Tokyo ni ikimasu* – I'm going to Tokyo

Go out

deru (*de-*) *demasu* (Group 2) ('te' form: *dete*)
  e.g. *Kanojo wa demashita ka* – Did she go out?

Have/has

1. In the normal sense of 'carrying' or 'possessing'
motteiru (*mottei-*) (Group 2) ('te' form: *motte*)
  e.g. *Kare wa kuruma wo motteimasuka* – Does he have a car?
  e.g. *Watashi wa pen wo motteimasu* – I have a pen

2. When not talking about possessions, as such, like in the sense of 'there is/are', or 'exists here'
iru (*i-*) *imasu* (living things)
  e.g. *Watashi niwa imouto ga hutari imasu* – I have 2 sisters (Really: "To me, sisters, there are two")
aru (*ari-*) *arimasu* (inanimate objects)
  e.g. *Sushi wa arimasuka* – Do you have sushi? (Really: "Is there sushi?")

Know

shiru (*shiri-*) *shirimasu* (Group 1) ('te' form: *shitte*)
  e.g. *Watashi wa shirimasen* – I don't know

Like

suki desu (follows conjugation of '*desu*')
  e.g. *Watashi wa chiizu ga suki dewa arimasen* – I don't like cheese
  e.g. *Anatatachi wa koora ga suki desuka* – Do you like coke?

Listen

kiku (*kiki-*) *kikimasu* (Group 1) ('te' form: *kiite*)
  e.g. *Anatatachi wa kikimasen deshita* – You (pl.) didn't listen

Look, watch, see

miru (*mi-*) *mimasu* (Group 2) ('te' form: *mite*)
  e.g. *Watashi wa sore wo mimasesn deshita* – I didn't see it
  e.g. *Kore wo mite kudasai* – Look at this, please

Love

aishiteiru (*aishitei-*) *aishiteimasu* (Group 2) ('te' form: *aishiteite*)
  e.g. *Kare wa sakkaa wo aishiteimasu* – He loves football (soccer)

Read

yomu (*yomi-*) *yomimasu* (Group 1) ('te' form: *yonde*)
  e.g. *(Watashi wa) manga wo yomimasen* – I don't read comics

Put

oku (*oki-*) (Group 1) ('te' form: *oite*)
  e.g. *Sono nomimono wo koko ni oite kudasai* – Put the drinks here, please

Speak

hanasu (hanashi-) hanashimasu (Group 1) ('te' form: *hanushite*)
  e.g. *(Anata wa) eigo wo hanashimasuka* – Do you speak English?
  e.g. *(Watashi wa) nihongo wo hanasemasen* – I can't speak Japanese

Sleep

neru (ne-) nemasu (Group 2) ('te' form: *nete*)
  e.g. *Karera wa nemasuka* – Are they sleeping?

Study

Benkyou suru (benkyou shi-) (Group 3) ('te' form: *benkyou shite*)
  e.g. *Anata wa benkyou shimashita ka* – Did you study?

Travel

Ryokou suru (ryokou shi-) (Group 3) ('te' form: *ryokou shite*)
  e.g. *Watashi wa Nihon ni ryokou shitai desu* – I want to travel to Japan

Understand

wakaru (wakari-) wakarimasu (Group 1) ('te' form: *wakatte*)
  e.g. *(Watashi wa) wakarimasen* – I don't understand

Wait

matsu (matsi-) machimasu (Group 1) ('te' form: *matte*)
  e.g. *Koko de matte kudasai* – Wait here, please

Want + noun

hoshii desu (follows conjugation of '*desu*')
  e.g. *Watashi wa kore ga hoshii desu* – I want this
(Note the construction for this: Person + *wa* – Desired object + *ga* – *hoshii desu*).

Want to + verb

Remember this is formed by changing the verb ending ('-*tai desu*') as was shown earlier. Look back to the note on 'Want to' in the section on verb forms if necessary.

Wear

kiru (ki-) kimasu (Group 2) ('te' form: *kite*)
  e.g. *Kanojo wa kimono wo kimasu* – She wears a kimono

Write

kaku (kaki-) kakimasu (Group 1) ('te' form: *kaite*)
  e.g. *Kare wa kanojo ni tegami wo kakimashita* – He wrote her a letter

6e. 'Desu' and its Forms

'Desu' is different to other verbs and its forms are different too. The ones presented here are the main ones.

1. Present / Future Tense (am, is, are, will be):

Verb Form: 'desu'   [dess]

She is healthy
Kanojo wa genki desu
[kah-noh-joh wah g'en-kee dess]

2. Negative of the Present / Future (isn't, aren't, won't be):

Verb Form: 'dewa arimasen'

She isn't healthy
Kanojo wa genki dewa arimasen
[kah-noh-joh wah g'en-kee deh-wah ah-ree-mah-sen]

3. Past Tense (was, were):

Verb Form: 'deshita'

She was healthy
Kanojo wa genki deshita
[kah-noh-joh wah g'en-kee deh-sh'tah]

4. Negative of the Past (wasn't, weren't):

Verb Form: 'dewa arimasen deshita'

She wasn't healthy
Kanojo wa genki dewa arimasen deshita
[kah-noh-joh wah g'en-kee deh-wah ah-ree-mah-sen deh-sh'tah]

5. Questions (are you, is he/she, will you be?):

As has already been shown, making questions in Japanese is just a case of adding '-ka' onto the end of the relevant form of the verb.

Verb Form (for present / future tense): *'desuka'*

Is she healthy?
Kanojo wa genki desuka
[kah-noh-joh wah g'en-kee dess-kah]

Of course, you can also add '*ka*' to the other verb forms:
Was she healthy?
Kanojo wa genki deshita ka
[kah-noh-joh wah g'en-kee deh-sh'tah kah]

7. Nouns

7a. General

Japanese nouns are fairly straightforward, but there are some things we need to note when using them.

A. Plurals

There is no change to the noun itself to make the plural (compare this to English where we normally add 's'). In fact, the plural is normally indicated by adding another word such as the following:

Nothing – When a noun is stated alone, it can mean either singular or plural. So to talk about e.g. 'cars' in general, you would just say, 'car' – doing this in Japanese can mean both singular and plural.

A Number – Using the number itself indicates the plural here. There is a more complex grammar point for this (an extra word needs to be added too), so see the Stating How Many section in the Numbers chapter.

A Plural Marker – For living things, there is a word that simply means 'plural'. This word is 'tachi', so for example, 'teacher' = '*sensei*', 'teachers' = '*sensei tachi*'; 'person' = '*hito*', 'people' = '*hito tachi*'; 'cat' = '*neko*', 'cats' = '*neko tachi*'. Remember that the same went for pronouns, 'I' = '*watashi*' and 'we' = '*watashitachi*').

An Indicator of Number – adding words like 'many' or 'few', which obviously indicate the plural themselves, in front of the noun.
Many   *takusan + no* + noun
(e.g. **Many apples** – *takusan no ringo* [tah-k'san noh rin-goh])

A few   *wazuka na* + noun
(e.g. **A few apples** – *wazuka na ringo* [wah-zuh-kah nah rin-goh])

B. Particles & Sentences

The same rules we learned for pronouns also go for nouns. So, where we said '*watashi wa*' to indicate the subject of the sentence, and '*watashi wo*' for the direct object, we would also do the same and say 'noun + *wa*' or 'noun + *wo*', and so on.

Let's quickly recap the 5 very important particles stated earlier for basic Japanese (We saw these in both the Sentences chapter and with the Pronouns, and here we will see them with nouns).

Also remember the word order presented earlier to make a basic Japanese sentence: Subject – Indirect Object – Direct Object – Extra Information – Verb. This structure will help you with your sentences in the beginning.

Subject / Topic: *wa*
The teacher thinks   ***Sensei wa*** *omoimasu.*
(*sensei* = teacher)

Indirect Object: *ni*
He gave it to the teacher   *Kare wa* ***sensei ni*** *sore wo agemashita.*
(*gakkou* = school)

Direct Object: *o*
The teacher has **a car**   *Sensei wa* ***kuruma wo*** *motteimasu.*
(*kuruma* = car)

Possessive: *no*
This is **the teacher's car**   *Kore wa* ***sensei no kuruma*** *desu.*
(*kuruma* = car)

Location: *ni*
The teacher went **to school**   *Sensei wa* ***gakkou ni*** *ikimashita.*
(*gakkou* = school)

Verb (to complete the sentence)
As shown in every one of the examples above, the verb comes at the end of the sentence.
The teacher **thinks**   *Sensei wa* ***omoimasu.***
The teacher **has** a car   *Sensei wa kuruma wo* ***motteimasu.***

7b. Some Common Nouns

People

Remember that the **plurals** of living things can be made simply by adding the word '*tachi*' after the noun.

Friend	*tomodachi*	[toh-moh-dah-chee]

(My friend = *watashi no tomodachi)*

Person	*hito*	[h'toh]
Boyfriend	*kareshi*	[kah-reh-shee]
Girlfriend	*kanojo*	[kah-noh-joh]
Husband	*otto*	[ot-toh]
Wife	*tsuma*	[ts'uh-mah]
Police	*keisatsukan*	[kay-sah-ts'kan]
Teacher	*sensei*	[sen-say]

Objects

Computer	*konpyuta*	[kon-pyuh-tah]
Telephone	*denwa*	[den-wah]
Watch	*tokei*	[toh-kay]
Book	*hon*	[hon]
Pen	*pen*	[pen]
Bag	*kaban*	[kah-ban]
Passport	*pasupoto*	[pass-(uh)-poh-toh]
Food	*tabemono*	[tah-beh-moh-noh]
Drink	*nomimono*	[noh-mee-moh-noh]

Places

Home	*ie*	[ee-eh]

(To go home = *ie ni kaeri masu)*

Work	*shigoto*	[shee-goh-toh]
Airport	*kuukou*	[kuuh-koh]
Guesthouse	*gesuto hausu*	[geh-s'toh how-suh]
Hotel	*hoteru*	[hoh-teh-ruh]

(My hotel is in Shinjuku – *Watashi no hoteru wa Shinjuku ni arimasu)*

Restaurant	*resutoran*	[reh-s'toh-ran]
Shop	*mise*	[mee-seh]
Convenience store	*konbini*	[kon-bee-nee]
School	*gakkou*	[gak-kou]
Park	*kouen*	[koh-en]
Toilet	*toire*	[toh'ee-reh]

Transport

Bicycle	*jitensya*	[jee-ten-s'yah]
Car	*kuruma*	[kuh-ruh-mah]
Taxi	*takushii*	[tah-k'shee]

Bus   *basu*   [bah'suh]
(Which bus goes to Shinjuku? – *Shinjuku iki no basu wa dore desuka)*

Train   *densya*   [den-s'yah]
(When is the **next train to Sapporo**? – ***Tsugi no Sapporo iki no densya*** *wa itsu desuka)*
(What platform does the train depart from? – *Densya wa nanban homu kara demasuka)*

Bus stop   *basutei*   [bah-s'tay]
Train Station   *eki*   [eh-kee]

Subway, metro   *chikatetsu*   [ch'kah-tet-suh]
Subway Station   *chikatetsu no eki*   [ch'kah-tet-suh noh eh-kee]
(I'm at the subway station – *watashi wa chikatetsu no eki ni imasu)*

8. Adjectives

8a. General

Japanese adjectives, as in English, come before the noun they describe (e.g. 'a new car') and there are no genders, but there are two types of adjective (known as '-*i*' adjectives and '-*na*' adjectives), and there are also different endings as we will see.

To get by in basic Japanese, we will consider the 3 main endings for the adjectives, which are used in the following 3 instances:
1. (adjective) + (noun) - e.g. A new car.
2. (noun) is (adjective) - e.g. The car is new.
3. (noun) is not (adjective) - e.g. The car isn't new.

First, we'll look at the adjective endings for each group with examples, and then we'll have a summary that you can commit to memory or refer back to. After that, there will be some common adjectives given in their groups and a quick exercise to practise using the endings.

Type 1: '-*i*' adjectives
'-*i*' adjectives work (somewhat) similarly to English adjectives when used in the positive, in that they can come before the noun ('a new car') or after as part of the larger sentence ('the car is new') without changing its ending. For the negative ('the car isn't new'), it is a case of changing the ending to '-*ku*' and changing the verb to a negative.

New   *atarashii*   [ah-tah-rah-shee]

A new car   No change
Atarashii kuruma   [ah-tah-rah-shee kuh-ruh-mah]

The (that) car is new   Just add '*desu*' for 'is'
Ano kuruma wa atarashii desu
[ah-noh kuh-ruh-mah wah ah-tah-rah-shee dess]

The (that) car is not new   Change '-*i*' to '-*ku*', then add '*arimasen*' for 'isn't'
Ano kuruma wa atarashiku arimasen
[ah-noh kuh-ruh-mah wah ah-tah-rah-sh'kuh ah-ree-mah-sen]

Type 2: '-na' adjectives

'-na' adjectives are basically 'loan words' – words that have come into Japanese from other languages, mostly from Chinese. With these, when the adjective is before the noun ('a pretty girl'), its ending remains as '-na', but this ending is dropped for 'Noun is/isn't Adjective', and you just need to add 'is' (desu) or 'isn't' (dewa arimasen) after the adjective since the verb goes at the end as usual.

Pretty *kirei (kireina)* [kee-ray, kee-ray-nah]

A pretty girl Add '-na'
Kireina onnanoko [kee-ray-nah on-nah-noh-koh]

She is pretty Just add 'desu' for 'is'
Kanojo wa kirei desu [kah-noh-joh wah kee-ray dess]

She is not pretty Just add 'dewa arimasen' for 'isn't'
Kanojo wa kirei dewa arimasen
[kah-noh-joh wah kee-ray deh-wah ah-ree-mah-sen]

SUMMARY

'-i' adjectives
Adjective + Noun: No change
Noun is Adjective: Add 'desu'
Noun isn't Adjective: Change '-i' to '-ku' then add 'arimasen'

'-na' adjectives
Adjective + Noun: Add '-na'
Noun is Adjective: Just add 'desu'
Noun isn't Adjective: Just add 'dewa arimasen'

8b. Some Common Adjectives

'-i' adjectives

Big	*ookii*	[oh-kee]
Small	*chiisai*	[chee-sigh]
New	*atarashii*	[ah-tah-rah-shee]
Old	*hurui*	[huh-ruh'ee]

Good	*yoi / ii*	[yoh'ee / ee]

(this is an exception, and becomes: *'ii desu'*, *'yoku arimasen'*)

Bad	*warui*	[wah-ruh'ee]

Cheap	*yasui*	[yah-suh'ee]
Expensive	*takai*	[tah-kye]

Hot	*atsui*	[at-suh'ee]
Cold (weather)	*samui*	[sah-muh'ee]
Cold (drink)	*tsumetai*	[ts'uh-meh-tie]

Near	*chikai*	[ch'kye]
Far	*tooi*	[toh'ee]

Beautiful	*utsukushii*	[uh-ts'kuh-shee]
Fun	*tanoshii*	[tah-noh-shee]
Delicious	*oishii*	[oh'ee-shee]
Spicy	*karai*	[kah-rye]

'-na' adjectives

Favourite	*suki (sukina)*	[s'kee(-nah)]
Healthy	*genki (genkina)*	[g'en-kee(-nah)]
Pretty	*kirei (kireina)*	[kee-ray(-nah)]
Quiet	*shizuka (shizukana)*	[shee-zuh-kah(-nah)]

Examples:

('*-i*')

A small boy	*Chiisai otokonoko*	[chee-sigh oh-toh-koh-noh-koh]
The boy is small	*Sono otokonoko wa chiisai desu*	
The boy isn't small	*Sono otokonoko wa chiisaku arimasen*	

('*-i*')

An old house	*Hurui ie*	[huh-ruh'ee ee-eh]
That old house is beautiful	*Ano hurui ie wa utsukushii desu*	
That old house isn't beautiful	*Ano hurui ie wa utsukushiku arimasen*	

('*-i*')

A spicy meal	*Karai ryori*	[kah-rye r'yoh-ree]
My meal is (very) spicy	*Watashi no ryori wa (totemo) karai desu*	
My meal isn't spicy	*Watashi no ryori wa karaku arimasen*	

('*-i*')

A new car	*Atarashii kuruma*	[ah-tah-rah-shee kuh-ruh-mah]
I want a new car	*Watashi wa atarashii kuruma ga hoshii desu*	

(Remember the construction for 'want + noun': Person *wa* + desired object *ga* + *hoshii desu*)

('*-na*')

A quiet person	*Shizukana hito*	[shee-zuh-kah-nah h'toh]
That person is quiet	*Sono hito wa shizuka desu*	
That person isn't quiet	*Sono hito wa shizuka dewa arimasen*	

Easy Practice
Cover the next page and see if you can translate these phrases. Then take a look at the next page to check your answers.

1. For the '*-i*' adjective, '*tsumetai*' (cold):

Cold coffee (coffee = '*koohii*')

My coffee ('*watashi no koohii*') **is cold**

My coffee isn't cold

2. For the '*-na*' adjective, '*genkina*' (healthy):

A healthy person (person = '*hito*')

That ('*sono*') **person is healthy**

That person isn't healthy

Easy Practice Answers

1. '*tsumetai*'
   Cold coffee   *Tsumetai koohii*   [ts'uh-meh-tie koh-hee]
   My coffee is cold   *Watashi no koohii wa tsumetai desu*
   My coffee isn't cold   *Watashi no koohii wa tsumetaku arimasen*

2. '*genkina*'
   A healthy person   *Genkina hito*   [g'en-kee-nah h'toh]
   That ('*sono*') person is healthy   *Sono hito wa genki desu*
   That person isn't healthy   *Sono hito wa genki dewa arimasen*

9. Questions & Question Words

Making questions in Japanese is extremely easy. Firstly, if you wish to turn a statement into a question, all you need to do is add '*ka*' to the end of the sentence (you can think of it like a question mark spoken out loud). For example, (Notice the use of '*arimasen*', because the sense is 'exists', so '*arimasu*', and not 'is equivalent to', which would be '*desu*'):

My watch is here
Watashi no tokei wa koko ni arimasu
[wah-tah-shee noh toh-kay wah koh-koh knee ah-ree-mass]

Is my watch here?
Watashi no tokei wa koko ni arimasu ka
[wah-tah-shee noh toh-kay wah koh-koh knee ah-ree-mass kah]

My watch was there
Watashi no tokei wa soko ni arimashita
[wah-tah-shee noh toh-kay wah soh-koh knee ah-ree-mah-sh'tah]

Was my watch there?
Watashi no tokei wa soko ni arimashita ka
[wah-tah-shee noh toh-kay wah soh-koh knee ah-ree-mah-sh'tah kah]

(my watch = *watashi no tokei*
[wah-tah-shee noh toh-kay])

The next thing, then, is how to use question words (what, where, who, why, when, how). This is also pretty easy in Japanese, and basically involves adding the question word after the sentence subject / topic, and still including the '*ka*' at the end of the sentence to indicate it is a question. For example,

<u>Where</u> is my watch?
Watashi no tokei wa <u>doko</u> ni arimasu ka
[wah-tah-shee noh toh-kay wah doh-koh knee ah-ree-mass kah]

<u>Why</u> is my watch here?
Watashi no tokei wa <u>doushite</u> koko ni arimasu ka
[wah-tah-shee noh toh-kay wah doh-sh'teh koh-koh knee ah-ree-mass kah]

However, one thing to note is that the question words are also followed by particles where necessary, as will be demonstrated in the examples.

So, with that basic knowledge of how to form questions in Japanese, let's see the question words themselves along with some examples of them in use. Just learn the list, and practise mixing the examples up a bit, substituting one word for another – this is basically all that's needed to change the questions.

The Question Words

What?

    Nani + most verbs Or: *Nan* + *'desu'* [nah-knee / nan]

'*Nani*' is followed by the particle '*ga*' if it is the subject, and '*wo*' if it is the direct object.

What is it?

Nan desu ka   [nan dess kah]

What's this / that?

Kore / sore wa nan desu ka [koh-reh / soh-reh wah nan dess kah]

What do you want?

Anata wa nani ga hoshii desu ka

[ah-nah-tah wah nah-knee gah hoh-shee dess kah]

Remember, in this case, the construction for 'want + noun': Noun + *ga* + *hoshii desu*

What do you want to drink?

(Anata wa) nani wo nomitai desu ka

[(ah-nah-tah wah) nah-knee woh noh-mee-tie dess kah]

What will she do?

Kanojo wa nani wo shimasu ka

[kah-noh-joh wah nah-knee woh shee-mass kah]

Who? *Dare* [dah-reh]

'*Dare*' is followed by the particle '*ga*' if it is the subject, and '*wo*' if it is the object.

Who is coming?

Dare ga kimasu ka   [dah-reh gah kee-mass kah]

Who wants to know?

Dare ga shiritai desu ka   [dah-reh gah shee-ree-tie dess kah]

57

Who did you see?
(Anata wa) dare wo mimashita ka
[(ah-nah-tah wah) dah-reh woh mee-mah-sh'tah kah]

Where? *Doko* [doh-koh]
'*Doko*' is followed by the particle '*ni*' (or '*de*'), to indicate that it refers to the location. The exception is when using '*desu*' – in this case, no particle is needed.

Where are you going?
(Anatatachi wa) doko ni ikimasuka
[(ah-nah-tah tah-chee wah) doh-koh knee ee-kee-mass-kah]
Note the use of '*ni*' – 'to where' are we going?

Where is your school?
Anata no gakkou wa doko desu ka
[ah-nah-tah noh gak-koh wah doh-koh dess kah]
Note there is no '*ni*' because the verb is '*desu*'

When? *Itsu* [ee-ts'uh]

When do you want to go?
(Anata wa) itsu ikitai desu ka
[(ah-nah-tah wah) ee-ts'uh ee-k'tie dess kah]

When did you see them?
(Anata wa) karera wo itsu mimashita ka
[(ah-nah-tah-wah) kah-reh-rah woh ee-ts'uh mee-mah-sh'tah kah]

Why? *Doushite* [doh-sh'teh]

Why don't you like him?
(Anata wa) doushite kare wo suki dewa arimasen ka
[(ah-nah-tah wah) doh-sh'teh kah-reh woh s'kee deh-wah ah-ree-mah-sen kah]

Why did they do that?
Karera wa doushite sore wo shimashita ka
[kah-reh-rah wah doh-sh'teh soh-reh woh shee'mah-sh'tah kah]

How? *Donoyouni* [doh-noh-yoh-knee]

How do you eat this?
Kore wo donoyouni tabemasu ka
[koh-reh woh doh-noh-yoh-knee tah-beh-mass kah]

How did you do that?
Sore wo donoyouni shimashita ka
[soh-reh woh doh-noh-yoh-knee shee-mah-sh'tah kah]

How much? *Ikura*

How much is it?
Ikura desuka　　　　　[ee-kuh-rah dess-kah]

10. Demonstratives (this, that, here, there)

There are a few things to note with 'this'/'that' & 'here'/'there' in Japanese.

- There are 3 words for 'this' and 'that' compared to our two in English. Japanese specifies whether it is close to the speaker, close to the listener, or far from both (i.e. 'over there'). First, 'here' and 'this', close to the speaker, which start with 'k-'. Then, 'there' and 'that', close to the listener which start with 's-'. Finally, 'over there' and 'that (over there)' which start with 'a-'. Additionally, each has a question word that begins with 'd-'.

- There are also 2 different kinds of 'this'/'that' in Japanese. Firstly, where we say 'this'/'that' without attaching it to a noun (Japanese: *kore, sore, are*), and secondly for 'this'/'that' plus a noun, e.g. 'this book' (Japanese: *kono* ___ , *sono* ___ , *ano* ___).

- Except when used with '*desu*', the words 'here' and 'there' are followed by the particle '*ni*', because they indicate a location. This will be shown in the examples for 'here' and 'there'.

'this' & 'that' _alone_ (i.e. not plus noun – e.g. **This** is a book)

This (near speaker)	*kore*	[koh-reh]
That (near listener)	*sore*	[soh-reh]
That (over there)	*are*	[ah-reh]
Which?	*dore*	[doh-reh]

e.g. **This is a book**   *Kore wa hon desu*
That is a computer   *Sore wa konpyuta desu*

'this' & 'that' + noun (e.g. This book is good)

This book (near speaker)	*kono hon*	[koh-noh (hon)]
That book (near listener)	*sono hon*	[soh-noh (hon)]
That book (over there)	*ano hon*	[ah-noh (hon)]
Which book?	*dono hon*	[doh-noh (hon)]

e.g. **This chair**   *kono isu*
That chair   *ano isu*
This chair is big   *Kono isu wa ookii desu*

'here' and 'there'

Here (near speaker)	*koko (ni)*	[koh-koh (knee)]
There (near listener)	*soko (ni)*	[soh-koh (knee)]
Over there	*asoko (ni)*	[ah-soh-koh (knee)]
Where?	*doko (ni)*	[doh-koh (knee)]

e.g. **Where is the book?**	*Hon wa doko desu ka*
The book is here	*Hon wa koko desu*

Now, when using any other verb (not '*desu*'), notice that the word '*ni*' follows the words for 'here', 'there' & 'where'.

Where are you going?	*Anata wa doko ni ikimasuka*
Please come here	*Koko ni kite kudasai*
There is a car over there	*Asoko ni kuruma ga arimasu*

(NB: As a more advanced Japanese point (skip over this if you are aiming for just 'getting by'), there is another word, '*de*', that can be added instead of '*ni*' – this is another good example of the subtle nuances in meaning between Japanese particles – they can both mean 'at', but if you use '*ni*', it stresses the place where it happens, and if you use '*de*', it stresses the action that is happening. So if it is the location that is more important: "He studies **here**", then it is really '*ni*', and if it is the action that is more important and the location is just stated as the place where it happens, then it is '*de*'. As mentioned, this is a bit more advanced than necessary for getting by, so it is up to you whether to stick with '*ni*' or remember both, e.g. "She sleeps there" (without stressing any word) – "*Kanojo wa asoko de nemasu*"; "No. She sleeps **here**" – "Iie. (*Kanojo wa) koko ni nemasu*").

11. Other Useful Words & Phrases

Answering Questions

Note about 'Yes' & 'No'

In Japanese, 'yes' and 'no' really mean "what you said is correct" or "what you said is not correct". This can lead to confusion if you are not aware of it. For positive sentences or agreeing, there is no issue, but when a negative question is asked or a negative statement is made, it is in English that we do something that could be seen as not making sense.

For example, if I say, "You don't want me to do that?" – in English, to say 'no', would be to agree that they don't want you to do that (as in, "No, I don't"). In Japanese, however, to say 'no' would actually be saying, "No, that is incorrect." – i.e. "That's incorrect. I do want you to do that". For us, it is because, when we say 'yes', we imagine it is followed by a positive statement ("Yes, I do"), and 'no' is short for a negative statement ("No, I don't"). For Japanese people (as well as other Asian nationalities) 'no' really means 'no' ('that's wrong'), and 'yes' really means just 'yes' (as in 'that's right').

This makes a lot of sense if you think about it, and whether it is Asian people learning English or English-speakers learning Asian languages, this is just something that everyone has to learn to get used to.

So basically, be aware of this, and try to consider '*hai*' and '*iie*' ('yes' and 'no') more as 'that's right / correct' and 'that's not right / that's incorrect'.

Yes / Correct	*hai*	[hi]
No / Incorrect	*iie*	[ee-eh]
Ok	*okkei / wakarimashita*	[ok-kay / wah-kah-ree-mah-sh'tah]
I don't know	*shirimasen*	[shee-ree-mah-sen]
I don't understand	*wakarimasen*	[wah-kah-ree-mah-sen]
Sorry	*gomennasai*	[goh-men-nah-sigh]
No problem	*daijoubudesu*	[die-joh-buh-dess]

Making Requests

Please *kudasai / onegaishimasu* [kuh-dah-sigh / oh-neh-guy-shee-mass]

This is very useful in Japanese, and the basic way to request something, is just to state:

{noun + *wo*} + **please**.

For example,

Water, please	*Mizu wo kudasai*	[mee-zuh woh kuh-dah-sigh]

Or you can include a number too (see the **Stating How Many** section for more details on this).

Two tickets, please *Chiketto* (tickets) *wo ni-mai kudasai*
[ch'ket-toh woh knee-my kuh-dah-sigh]

Three bowls of rice, please *Gohan* (rice) *wo san-bai kudasai*
[goh-han woh san-bye kuh-dah-sigh]

Modifying

Too ...*sugi* [soo-ghee]
  e.g. *oo sugi* = too much

Very *totemo*... [toh-teh-moh]
  e.g. *totemo ookii* = very big

Quite *kanari*... [kah-nah-ree]
  e.g. *kanari takai* = quite expensive

Distinguishing

A lot, many *takusan no* + noun [tah-k'san noh...]
A few, a little *wazuka na* + noun [wah-zuh-kah na...]

Time Vocab

Today *kyou* [k'yoh]
Tomorrow *ashita* [ah-sh'tah]
Yesterday *kinou* [kee-noh]
The day after tomorrow *asatte* [ah-sat-teh]
The day before yesterday *ototoi* [oh-toh-toh'ee]
Now *ima* [ee-mah]

Location
At, in, on, to *ni* [knee]
  (Tom is at the hotel – *Tomu wa hoteru ni imasu* [toh-muh wah hoh-teh-ruh knee ee-mass])

12. Numbers & Counting

12a. General

Basic numbers in Japanese are quite easy if you memorise the first 10 since, like in English, larger numbers are based on these 10, but note that there are 2 forms for numbers 4, 7 & 9, which are used in different situations.

1-10

(0	*rei / zero)*	[ray, zeh-roh]
1	*ichi*	[ee-chee]
2	*ni*	[knee]
3	*san*	[san]
4	*shi / yon*	[shee, yon]
5	*go*	[goh]
6	*roku*	[roh-kuh]
7	*nana / shichi*	[nah-nah, sh'chee]
8	*hachi*	[hah-chee]
9	*kyuu / ku*	[k'yuuh, kuh]
10	*juu*	[juuh]

Nos. 4, 7 & 9: It is a case here of just learning what is used in which situation.
4 (*shi/yon*), 4 o'clock (*yo-ji*), 4 years old (*yon-sai*)
7 (*nana/shichi*), 7 o'clock (*shichi-ji*), 7 years old (*nana-sai*)
9 (*kyuu/ku*), 9 o'clock (*ku-ji*), 9 years old (*kyuu-sai*)

11-99
From 11-99, the numbers are easy because they are simply stated as follows:

12	**"ten two"**	*juu ni*	[juuh knee]
14	**"ten four"**	*juu yon*	[juuh yon]
15	**"ten five"**	*juu go*	[juuh goh]
17	**"ten seven"**	*juu nana*	[juuh nah-nah]
19	**"ten nine"**	*juu kyuu*	[juuh k'yuuh]
20	**"two ten"**	*ni juu*	[knee juuh]
23	**"two ten three"**	*ni juu san*	[knee juuh san]
30	**"three ten"**	*san juu*	[san juuh]
54	**"five ten four"**	*go juu yon*	[goh juuh yon]
78	**"seven ten eight"**	*nana juu hachi*	[nah-nah juuh hah-chee]

Hundreds & Thousands

To count in hundreds is slightly different, in that when stating multiple hundreds, the form of the number changes. So first, let's see the words for the 'hundreds', and then a couple of examples of how to use them.

100	*hyaku*	[h'yah-kuh]
200	*nihyaku*	[knee h'yah-kuh]
300	*sanbyaku*	[san-b'yah-kuh]
400	*yonhyaku*	[yon-h'yah-kuh]
500	*gohyaku*	[goh-h'yah-kuh]
600	*roppiaku*	[rop-p'yah-kuh]
700	*nanahyaku*	[nah-nah-h'yah-kuh]
800	*happyaku*	[hap-yah-kuh]
900	*kyuuhyaku*	[k'yuuh h'yah-kuh]

124   **"One hundred two ten four"**
Hyaku-nijuu-yon / hyaku-nijuu-shi

150   **"One hundred five ten"**
Hyaku-gojuu

648   **"Six hundred four ten eight"**
Roppiaku-yonjuu-hachi

Then, the thousands are as follows:

1,000	*sen*	[sen]
2,000	*nisen*	[knee-sen]
3,000	*sanzen*	[san-zen]
4,000	*yonsen*	[yon-sen]
5,000	*gosen*	[goh-sen]
6,000	*rokusen*	[roh-k'sen]
7,000	*nanasen*	[nah-nah-sen]
8,000	*hassen*	[hass-sen]
9,000	*kyuusen*	[k'yuuh-sen]
1,500	*sen-gohyaku*	[sen-goh-h'yah-kuh]
4,750	*yonsen-nanahyaku-gojuu*	
	[yon-sen-nah-nah h'yah-kuh goh-juuh]	

12b. Higher Numbers in Japanese

Higher numbers are considered and stated differently in Japanese. Whereas in English, our numbers keep going up in tens, hundreds, thousands, and then millions, Japanese also has a term for 10,000 ("*man*"). So higher numbers in Japanese become based on this number. You can think of this number as having four 0's, i.e. "1,0000".

So for example, where we say 20,000, in Japanese, this will be "2 ten thousands". The Japanese for 100,000, is "10 ten thousands", and for one million, the Japanese equivalent is "100 ten thousands". This can be confusing (mathematically!) for us, but is just one of those things that you have to get your head round over time, and will only have an effect on you if you find yourself wanting to say these larger numbers – in practice, we don't tend to say these numbers that often anyway.

10,000   **"one ten thousand / 1,0000"**
ichi-man   [ee-chee man]

20,000   **"two ten thousands / 2,0000"**
ni-man   [knee-man]

25,000   **"two ten thousands, five thousand / 2,5000"**
niman-gosen   [knee-man goh-sen]

100,000   **"10 ten thousands / 10,0000"**
juu-man   [juuh-man]

650,000   **"sixty-five ten thousands / 65,0000"**
rokujuu go-man   [roh-kuh juuh goh-man]

1,000,000   **"100 ten thousands / 100,0000"**
hyaku-man   [h'yah-kuh man]

Easy Practice
Cover the answers on the next page, and work out these numbers in Japanese. Then check against the answers given: 250, 725, 932, 3575.

Easy Practice Answers

250   *nihyaku-gojuu*   [knee-h'yah-kuh goh-juuh]

725   *nanahyaku-nijuu-go*   [nah-nah-h'yah-kuh knee-juuh goh]

932   *kyuuhyaku-sanjuu-ni*   [k'yuuh-h'yah'kuh san-juuh-knee]

3575   *sanzen-gohyaku-nanajuu-go*
                              [san-zen goh-h'yah-kuh nah-nah-juuh goh]

12c. Stating how many

In English, to state 'how many' of something, it is simply a case of saying: Number + Noun (sing. or pl.).

Unfortunately, it is not quite so simple in Japanese. Japanese has something called 'counter words', which indicate what kind of noun you are talking about. We do have something like this in English, e.g. 'bottles', 'cans', 'sheets', which we insert between the number and the noun.

In English, we are used to saying, e.g. "2 bottles of water" or "50 sheets of paper" and so on. The thing in Japanese, is that this basically goes for all nouns, and there are many different counter words, meaning various things, like 'bottle' (as in English), but also things like 'flat thing', 'long cylindrical thing' and 'small round thing' among others. This means that the Japanese say "2 bottles of water" just as we do, but they also say, for example, "4 long cylinder-ish things of pens" and "3 flat things of books".

This might sound a bit complicated (and it can be!), but there is a step to take that can ease us into stating how many in Japanese. The traditional numerals in Japanese can be used in place of counter words for many kinds of noun (i.e. if you do not know the correct word, you can use these numerals – although they will be wrong in some instances, for example they cannot be used to count people).

So first, we will learn these numerals along with some examples of their use, and then move onto the actual counter words and how to use them.

Tsu: Objects of random shape or which do not fit in to the other categories

In reality, these below are actually the traditional Japanese numerals, while the ones covered earlier are related to Chinese. The below can be used to replace the proper counter words for various objects, and are typically used for quite small objects of various shapes. As already stated, this can be a fall-back option if you can't remember the actual counter words, and will be enough to get you by and be understood in most instances.

1	_hitotsu_	[h'toh-ts'uh]
2	_hutatsu_	[h'tah-ts'uh]
3	_mittsu_	[mit-ts'uh]
4	_yottsu_	[yot-ts'uh]
5	_itsutsu_	[ee-ts'uh-ts'uh]
6	_muttsu_	[muh't-ts'uh]
7	_nanatsu_	[nah-nah-ts'uh]
8	_yattsu_	[yat-ts'uh]
9	_kokonotsu_	[koh-koh-noh-ts'uh]
10	_tou_	[toh]

Also to learn, 'how many' and 'some', which will be included for each counter word (mostly easy to learn).

How many?   *Nanmai?*   [nan-my]
Some   *nanmaika*   [nan-my-kah]

When you count objects using these numbers, the word order is different to English. In English, we just say, "5 apples" or "I have 2 pens". In Japanese, however, the noun comes first, then the number, then the verb. So:

Noun – Number – Verb

5 apples   **"Apples, 5"**
Ringo itsutsu   [rin-goh ee-ts'uh-ts'uh]

I have 2 watches   **"Watches, 2, I have"**
Tokei wo hutatsu motteimasu   [toh-kay woh h'tah-ts'uh mot-tay-mass]

I want one   **"One, please"**
Hitotsu kudasai   [h'toh-ts'uh kuh-dah-sigh]

Ok, so that's counting with the traditional Japanese numerals, and remember these can be used if you are stuck and you will be understood (although it won't always be correct to use them).

Requesting things by numbers
This has been shown earlier, but now to give the examples again armed with the knowledge of how to state how many in Japanese as well.

To request something in Japanese using the numbers like this, you say:
Noun + *wo* – Number + Counter Word – Please

For example,
I want one   *Hitotsu kudasai*   [h'toh-ts'uh kuh-dah-sigh]

Two tickets, please   *Chiketto* (tickets) *wo ni-mai kudasai*
                                   [ch'ket-toh woh knee-my kuh-dah-sigh]

Three bowls of rice, please   *Gohan wo san-bai kudasai*
                                   [goh-han woh san-bye kuh-dah-sigh]

Useful Counter Words

Ko: Small, compact items (pebble, apple, eraser)

1	*ikko*	[ik-koh]
2	*niko*	[knee-koh]
3	*sanko*	[san-koh]
4	*yonko*	[yon-koh]
5	*goko*	[goh-koh]
6	*rokko*	[rok-koh]
7	*nanako*	[nah-nah-koh]
8	*hakko*	[hak-koh]
9	*kyuuko*	[k'yuuh-koh]
10	*jukko*	[juh'k-koh]

Then

11	*juuikko*	[juuh-ik-koh]
12	*juuniko*	[juuh-knee-koh]
16	*juurokko*	[juuh-rok-koh]
18	*juuhakko*	[juuh-hak-koh]
20	*nijukko*	[knee-juuh-koh]

How many?	*Nanko?*	[nan-koh]
Some	*nankoka*	[nan-koh-kah]
Many	*takusan no* (+ noun)	[tah-k'san noh]
A few	*wazuka na* (+ noun)	[wah-zuh-kah nah]

Using some of the same examples we saw above, but changed to use the true counter word:

5 apples   **"Apples, 5"**
Ringo goko   [rin-goh goh-koh]

I have 2 apples   **"Apples, 2, I have"**
Ringo wo niko motteimasu   [rin-goh woh knee-koh mot-tay-mass]

One apple, please   **"Apples, 1, please"**
Ringo wo ikko kudasai   [rin-goh woh ik-koh kuh-dah-sigh]

I have some apples   **"Apples, some, I have"**
Ringo wo nankoka motteimasu   [rin-goh woh nan-koh-kah mot-tay-mass]

How many apples do you have? **"Apples, how many, do you have?"**
Ringo wo nanko motteimasuka   [rin-goh woh nan-koh mot-tay-mass-kah]

Nin: People

1	_hitori_	[h'toh-ree]
2	_hutari_	[h'tah-ree]
3	_san-nin_	[san-nin]
4	_yo-nin_	[yoh-nin]
5	_go-nin_	[goh-nin]
6	_roku-nin_	[roh-kuh-nin]
7	_shichi-nin_	[sh'chee-nin]
8	_hachi-nin_	[hah-chee-nin]
9	_kyuu-nin_	[k'yuuh-nin]
10	_juu-nin_	[juuh-nin]

How many?	_Nannin?_	[nan-nin]
Some	_nanninka_	[nan-nin-kah]
Many	_takusan no hito_	[tah-k'san noh h'toh]
A few	_wazuka na hito_	[wah-zuh-kah nah h'toh]

There are six people   **"6 people, there are"**
Roku-nin imasu [roh-kuh-nin ee-mass]
Note that 'people' is strongly conveyed by the word '_nin_' so the actual noun for person is not required here.

Hon/pon: Long, cylindrical items (pencil, pole, stick, tree, bottle)

1	_ip-pon_	[ip-pon]
2	_ni-hon_	[knee-hon]
3	_san-bon_	[san-bon]
4	_yon-hon_	[yon-hon]
5	_go-hon_	[goh-hon]
6	_rop-pon_	[rop-pon]
7	_nana-hon_	[nah-nah-hon]
8	_hap-pon_	[hap-pon]
9	_kuu-hon_	[kuuh-hon]
10	_jup-pon_	[juh'p-pon]

How many?	_Nanbon?_	[nan-bon]
Some	_nanbonka_	[nan-bon-kah]
Many	_takusan no_ (+ noun)	[tah-k'san noh]
A few	_wazuka na_ (+ noun)	[wah-zuh-kah nah]

4 bottles of water
Yon-hon no mizu   [yon-hon noh mee-zuh]

4 bottles of water, please
Yon-hon no mizu wo kudasai   [yon-hon noh mee-zuh kuh-dah-sigh]

Mai: Thin items (paper, bill, leaf)

1	_ichi-mai_	[ee-chee-my]
2	_ni-mai_	[knee-my]
3	_san-mai_	[san-my]
4	_yon-mai_	[yon-my]
5	_go-mai_	[goh-my]
6	_roku-mai_	[roh-kuh-my]
7	_nana-mai_	[nah-nah-my]
8	_hachi-mai_	[hah-chee-my]
9	_kyuu-mai_	[k'yuuh-my]
10	_juu-mai_	[juuh-my]

How many?	_Nanmai?_	[nan-my]
Some	_nanmaika_	[nan-my-kah]
Many	_takusan no_ (+ noun)	[tah-k'san noh]
A few	_wazuka na_ (+ noun)	[wah-zuh-kah nah]

Two tickets, please   _Chiketto_ (tickets) _wo ni-mai kudasai_
[ch'ket-toh woh knee-my kuh-dah-sigh]

Bai: bowls, plates, cups, glasses of food & drink

1	_ippai_	[ip-pie]
2	_nihai_	[knee-high]
3	_sanbai_	[san-bye]
4	_yonhai_	[yon-high]
5	_go-hai_	[goh-high]
6	_roppai_	[rop-pie]
7	_nanahai_	[nah-nah-high]
8	_happai_	[hap-pie]
9	_kyuuhai_	[k'yuuh-high]
10	_juppai_	[juh'p-pie]

How many?	_Nanbai?_	[nan-bye]
Some	_nanbaika_	[nan-bye-kah]
Many	_takusan no_ (+ noun)	[tah-k'san noh]
A few	_wazuka na_ (+ noun)	[wah-zuh-kah nah]

Satsu: Book

1	*is-satsu*	[iss-sah-ts'uh]
2	*ni-satsu*	[knee-sah-ts'uh]
3	*san-satsu*	[san-sah-ts'uh]
4	*yon-satsu*	[yon-sah-ts'uh]
5	*go-satsu*	[goh-sah-ts'uh]
6	*roku-satsu*	[roh-kuh-sah-ts'uh]
7	*nana-satsu*	[nah-nah-sah-ts'uh]
8	*has-satsu / hachi-satsu*	[hass-sah-ts'uh / hah-chee-sah-ts'uh]
9	*kuu-satsu*	[kuuh-sah-ts'uh]
10	*jus-satsu*	[juh'ss-sah-ts'uh]

How many?	*Nan-satsu?*	[nan-sah-ts'uh]
Some	*nan-satsuka*	[nan-sat-s'kah]
Many	*takusan no hon* (books)	[tah-k'san noh hon]
A few	*wazuka na hon* (books)	[wah-zuh-kah nah]

Machinery (TV, computer, car)

1	*ichi-dai*	[ee-chee-die]
2	*ni-dai*	[knee-die]
3	*san-dai*	[san-die]
4	*yon-dai*	[yon-die]
5	*go-dai*	[goh-die]
6	*roku-dai*	[roh-kuh-die]
7	*nana-dai*	[nah-nah-die]
8	*hachi-dai*	[hah-chee-die]
9	*kuu-dai*	[kuuh-die]
10	*juu-dai*	[juuh-die]

How many?	*Nandai?*	[nan-die]
Some	*nandaika*	[nan-die-kah]
Many	*takusan no* (+ noun)	[tah-k'san noh]
A few	*wazuka na* (+ noun)	[wah-zuh-kah nah]

Kai: Floor / times

1	*ik-kai*	[ik-kye]
2	*ni-kai*	[knee-kye]
3	*san-kai*	[san-kye]
4	*yon-kai*	[yon-kye]
5	*go-kai*	[goh-kye]
6	*rok-kai*	[rok-kye]
7	*nana-kai*	[nah-nah-kye]
8	*hak-kai*	[hah-kye]
9	*kyuu-kai*	[k'yuuh-kye]
10	*juk-kai*	[juh'k-kye]

How many?	*Nankai?*	[nan-kye]
Some	*nankaika*	[nah-nah-kye-kah]
Many	*takusan no* + noun	[tah-k'san noh]
A few	*wazuka na* + noun	[wah-zuh-kah nah]

I have visited there 3 times
Watashi wa soko ni sankai ikimashita
[wah-tah-shee wah soh-koh knee san-kye ee-kee-mah-sh'tah]

Ages

1	*issai*	[iss-sigh]
2	*nisai*	[knee-sigh]
3	*sansai*	[san-sigh]
4	*yonsai*	[yon-sigh]
5	*gosai*	[goh-sigh]
6	*rokusai*	[roh-kuh-sigh]
7	*nanasai*	[nah-nah-sigh]
8	*hassai*	[hass-sigh]
9	*kyuusai*	[k'yuuh-sigh]
10	*jussai*	[juh'ss-sigh]
11	*juuissai*	[juuh-iss-sigh]
12	*juunisai*	[juuh-knee-sigh]
20	*nijussai / hatachi*	[knee-juuh-sigh / hah-tah-chee]

| **How old?** | *Nansai?* | [nan-sigh] |

12d. Telling the time

Just like in English, there are two methods of telling the time in Japanese (one is 'digital', like 5:20 or "five-twenty", and the second is using the words 'past' and 'to', as in "ten past five'). Both methods are fairly straightforward, again like they are in English.

Note that, for numbers 4, 7 & 9, the numbers used for telling the time are the second ones in the list we saw before. So, 4 = 'yon' (sometimes 'yo'), 7 = 'shichi', and 9 = 'ku'.

Asking: **What time is it?**
Ima, nan-ji desuka?   [ee-mah nan-jee dess-kah]

At + time: To say "At..." a certain time, just add '*ni*' after the time in Japanese
1:00   *ichi-ji*
At 1:00   *ichi-ji ni*

First Method: Digital Times (e.g. 5:20 or "five-twenty")

This is quite simple. First, just state the hour followed by the word '*ji*' to denote 'o'clock' and then the number of minutes followed by '*hun / pun*' (meaning minutes).

Hours
1:00	*ichi-ji*	[ee-chee jee]
2:00	*ni-ji*	[knee jee]
3:00	*san-ji*	[san jee]
4:00	*yo-ji*	[yoh jee]
5:00	*go-ji*	[goh jee]
6:00	*roku-ji*	[roh-kuh jee]
7:00	*shichi-ji*	[sh'chee jee]
8:00	*hachi-ji*	[hah-chee jee]
9:00	*ku-ji*	[kuh jee]
10:00	*juu-ji*	[juuh jee]
11:00	*juuichi-ji*	[juuh-ee-chee jee]
12:00	*juuni-ji*	[juuh-knee jee]

Minutes
5	*go-hun*	[goh-huh'n]
10	*juppun*	[juh'p-puh'n]
15	*juu go-hun*	[juuh goh-huh'n]
20	*ni-juppun*	[knee juh'p-puh'n]
25	*ni-juu go-hun*	[knee-juuh goh-huh'n]

75

30	*san-juppun*	[san-juh'p-puh'n]
35	*san-juu go-hun*	[san-juuh goh-huh'n]
40	*yon-juppun*	[yon-juh'p-puh'n]
45	*yon-juu go-hun*	[yon-juuh goh-huh'n]
50	*go-juppu*	[goh-juh'p-puh'n]
55	*go-juu go-hun*	[goh-juuh-goh-huh'n]

Examples

1:00 "1 o'clock"
ichi-ji   [ee-chee jee]

1:25 "1 o'clock 25 minutes"
ichi-ji ni-juu go-hun   [ee-chee jee knee-juuh goh huh'n]

7:20 "7 o'clock 20 minutes"
shichi-ji ni-juppun   [sh'chee jee knee juh'p-puh'n]

and so on...

<u>Second Method: Using 'past' & 'to'</u> (e.g. "ten past five")

You can make do with the method above, but if you want to know more, then the second way to tell the time is simple too, although things are slightly differently ordered than in English. Where we say, "ten past five", in Japanese this becomes, "5 o'clock, ten minutes past" (the 'past' or 'to' comes at the very end). In Japanese, this is used mainly for **5** and **10 minutes, past & to**. You may sometimes hear others, e.g. 25 minutes past, but it is not the norm.

So first, the Japanese words for 'past' and 'to' are:

Past	*sugi*	[suh-ghee]
To	*mae*	[mah-eh]

Then, the time is constructed as follows:

5 past 7 "7 o'clock 5 minutes past"
Shichi-ji go-hun sugi   [sh'chee-jee goh-huh'n suh-ghee]

5 to 7 "7 o'clock 5 minutes to"
Shichi-ji go-hun mae   [sh'chee-jee go-huh'n mah-eh]

10 past 5 "5 o'clock 10 minutes past"
Go-ji juppun sugi   [goh-jee juh'p-puh'n suh-ghee]

10 to 5   "5 o'clock 10 minutes to"
Go-ji juppun mae   [goh-jee juh'p-puh'n mah-eh]

To say 'quarter past / to'
There is no special word used for 'quarter' with Japanese times, so you may hear, '15 minutes past / to', and so it works the same as the times above.

Quarter past 5   "5 o'clock 15 minutes past"
Go-ji juugo-hun sugi   [goh-jee juuh-goh-huh'n suh-ghee]

Quarter to 6   "6 o'clock 15 minutes to"
Roku-ji juugo-hun mae   [roh-kuh-jee juuh-goh huh'n mah-eh]

To say 'half past'
To say 'half past' in Japanese, you just need to add the word '*han*' (half) after the hour. This means that to say, e.g. "Half past 5", means just saying the number of the hour, followed by '*ji*' (o'clock), followed by '*han*' (half):

Half past 5   "5 o'clock half"
Go-ji han   [goh-jee han]

Half past 6   "6 o'clock half"
Roku-ji han   [roh-kuh-jee han]

To Add A.M. or P.M.
If you wish to add 'A.M.' or 'P.M.', note that these words come **before** the time in Japanese (compared to English where they come **after** the time).

A.M.	*gozen*	[goh-zen]
P.M.	*gogo*	[goh-goh]

For example,

5:00 a.m.	*gozen go-ji*	[goh-zen goh-jee]
5:00 p.m.	*gogo go-ji*	[goh-goh goh-jee]

Easy Practice
Work out these times using both methods above (digitally, and using 'past' & 'to' where possible), then look over the page to see the answers.
6:30 a.m., 9:45a.m., 3:10 p.m., 5:35 p.m., 11:00 p.m.

Easy Practice Answers

6:30 a.m.
Gozen roku-ji han   [goh-zen roh-kuh-jee han]

9:55a.m.
Gozen ku-ji go-juu go-hun   [goh-zen kuh-jee goh-juuh goh-huh'n]

Or:
5 to 10
Juu-ji go-hun mae   [(go-zen) juuh-jee goh-huh'n mah-eh]

3:10 p.m.
Gogo san-ji juppun   [goh-goh san-jee juh'p-puh'n]

Or:
10 past 3
San-ji juppun sugi   [(goh-goh) san-jee juh'p-puh'n suh-ghee]

5:35 p.m.
Gogo go-ji san-juu go-hun   [goh-goh goh-jee san-juuh goh-huh'n]

11:00 p.m.
   Gogo juuichi-ji   [goh-goh juuh-ee-chee-jee]

PHRASES & CONVERSATION

13. Basic Conversation Questions and How to Answer Them

It is not too hard to get by in basic conversation in Japan if you know some basic questions and how to answer them. You will naturally pick up more once you start speaking.

1. **How are you?**   *Genki desuka*

2. **What's your name?**   *Onamae wa nandesuka*

3. **How old are you?**   *Nansai desuka*

4. **Where are you from?**   *Syusshin wa dokodesuka*

5. **Are you married?**   *Kekkon shiteimasuka*

6. **What do you do?**   *Oshigoto wa nandesuka*

7. **Where do you live?**   *Doko ni sunde imasuka*

8. **Do you like... (Japan)?** *...(Nihon) ga suki desuka*

1. How are you?
Genki desuka   [g'en-kee-dess-kah]

I am fine, thanks.
Hai genki desu   [hi g'en-kee-dess]

And you?
Anata wa   [ah-nah-tah wah]

2. What's your name?
Onamae wa nandesuka   [oh-nah-mah-eh wa nan-dess-kah]

My name's _____
Watashi no namae wa ___ desu
[wah-tah-shee noh nah-mah-eh wah ___ dess]

What about you?
Anata no onamae wa
[ah-nah-tah noh oh nah-mah-eh wah]

3. How old are you?
Nansai desuka   [nan-sigh dess-kah]

I am (21)
Watashi wa (nijuu-issai) desu
[wah-tah-shee wah (knee-juuh iss-sigh) dess]

I am (35)
Watashi wa (sanjuu-gosai) desu
[wah-tah-shee wah (san-juuh goh-sigh) dess]

What about you?
Anata wa   [ah-nah-tah wah]

4. Where are you from?
Syusshin wa dokodesuka   [s'yuh'ss-shin wah doh-koh dess-kah]

The formula to say where you are from is as follows:

I (country) person am
Watashi wa (...)-jin desu   [wah-tah-shee wah (...) jin dess]

e.g. **I am an English person**
Watashi wa Igirisujin desu
[wah-tah-shee wah ee-ghee-ree-suh jin dess]

Are you Japanese?
Anata wa Nihonjin desuka
[ah-nah-tah wah knee-hon jin dess-kah]

A short list of countries is below. If your country is not on here, ask someone when you arrive, e.g. at your hotel, how to say it, or look it up in this online Japanese dictionary (http://www.docoja.com/). As shown just above, to convert any country into the person from that country, just add '*-jin*' onto the end, e.g. **England** – *Igirisu*, **English person** – *Igirisujin*, **USA** – *Amerika*, **American** – *Amerikajin*.

Japan	*Nihon*	[knee-hon]
(Japanese person:	*Nihonjin*)	
England	*Igirisu*	[ee-ghee-ree-suh]
(English person:	*Igirisujin*)	
USA	*Amerika*	[ah-meh-ree-kah]
Canada	*Kanada*	[kah-nah-dah]
Australia	*Oosutoraria*	[oh-s'toh-rah-ree'ah]
Ireland	*Airurando*	[eye-ruh-ran-doh]
Germany	*Doitsu*	[doh'ee-ts'uh]
France	*Huransu*	[huh-ran-suh]
Italy	*Itaria*	[ee-tah-ree'ah]
Spain	*Supein*	[s'pain]
Russia	*Roshia*	[roh-shee'ah]
China	*Chuugoku*	[chuuh-goh-kuh]

To state which city you are from, you can say:
...syusshin desu   [...s'yuh'ss-shin dess]

Do you speak ... (language)?   *...o hanashimasuka*

English	*Eigo*	[ay-goh]
Japanese	*Nihongo*	[knee-hon-goh]
German	*Doitsugo*	[doh'ee-ts'uh-goh]
French	*Huransugo*	[huh-ran-suh-goh]
Italian	*Iratiago*	[ee-tah-ree'ah-goh]
Spanish	*Supeingo*	[s'pain-goh]
Russian	*Roshiago*	[roh-shee'ah-goh]
Chinese	*Chuugokugo*	[chuuh-goh-kuh -goh]

I can speak (a little) {Japanese}
Watashi wa {nihongo} wo (sukoshi) hanasemasu
[wah-tah-shee wah ___ woh (s'koh-shee) hah-nah-seh-mass]

I'm learning {Japanese}
Watashi wa {nihongo} wo naratte imasu
[wah-tah-shee wah ___ woh nah-rat-teh ee-mass]

No, I can't speak {Japanese}
{Nihongo} wo hanasemasen
[___ woh hah-nah-seh-mah-sen]

5. Are you married?
Kekkon shiteimasuka [kek-kon sh'tay-mass-kah]

Note that the above question can be taken as impolite by some people, but be prepared in case you are asked yourself.

I'm single
Watashi wa dokushin desu [wah-tah-shee wah doh-k'shin dess]

I'm married
Watashi wa kekkon shiteimasu [wah-tah-shee wah kek-kon sh'tay-mass]

This is my husband
Kochira wa watashi no otto desu
[koh-chee-rah wah wah-tah-shee noh ot-toh dess]

This is my wife
Kochira wa watashi no tsuma desu
[koh-chee-rah wah wah-tah-shee noh ts'uh-mah dess]

I have a boyfriend
Kareshi ga imasu [kah-reh-shee gah ee-mass]

I have a girlfriend
Kanojo ga imasu [kah-noh-joh gah ee-mass]

....

Do you have children?
Okosan wa imasuka [oh-koh-san wah ee-mass-kah]

I have 2 children
Kodomo ga hutari imasu [koh-doh-moh gah h'tah-ree ee-mass]

1 son and 1 daughter
Musuko ga hitori musume ga hitori desu
[muh-suh'k gah h'toh-ree muh'suh'meh gah h'toh-ree dess]

I don't have children
Kodomo wa imasen [koh-doh-moh wah ee-mah-sen]

6. What do you do?
Oshigoto wa nandesuka   [oh-shee-goh-toh nan-dess-kah]

This is where you will have to look up your own occupation – here is one online Japanese dictionary which gives the words both in Japanese and in our alphabet so you will be able to actually read them: **http://www.docoja.com/**

I am (a teacher)
Watashi wa sensei desu   [wah-tah-shee wah sen-say dess]

I am (a student)
Watashi wa gakusei desu   [wah-tah-shee wah gah-k'say dess]

7. Where do you live?
Doko ni sunde imasuka   [doh-koh knee suh'n-deh ee-mass-kah]

I live in Tokyo
Watashi wa Tokyo ni sunde imasu
[wah-tah-shee wah toh-k'yoh knee suh'n-deh ee-mass]

I live in America
Watashi wa Amerika ni sunde imasu
[wah-tah-shee wah ah-meh-ree-kah knee suh'n-deh ee-mass]

8. Do you like... (Japan)?
(Nihon)...ga suki desuka   [... gah s'kee dess-kah]

Yes, I do
Hai suki desu   [high s'kee dess]

No, I don't
Iie suki dewa arimasen   [ee-eh s'kee deh-wah ah-ree-mah-sen]

I love (Japan)
Nihon wo aishiteimasu   [knee-hon woh eye-sh'tay-mass]

I like (Japanese food)
(Nihon no ryouri) wa suki desu   [(knee-hon woh r'yoh-ree) wah s'kee dess]

I don't like...
...wa suki dewa arimasen   [...wah s'kee deh'wah ah-ree-mah-sen]

14. Situational Japanese

In a Taxi

Directing the Taxi

Go to...
...*ni itte kudasai*   [... knee it-teh kuh-dah-sigh]

Turn right
Migi ni magatte kudasai   [mee-ghee knee mah-gat-teh kuh-dah-sigh]

Turn left
Hidari ni magatte kudasai   [hee-dah-ree knee mah-gatt-teh kuh-dah-sigh]

Go straight
Massugu itte kudasai   [mass-suh-guh it-teh kuh-dah-sigh]

Stop here
Koko de tomatte kudasai   [koh-koh deh toh-mat-teh kuh-dah-sigh]

Here   *koko (ni / de)*   [koh-koh]
There   *soko (ni / de)*   [doh-koh]
Then   *sorekara*   [soh-reh-kah-rah]

Turn around or **Do a u-turn**
Utaan site kudasai   [uh-tah'n see-teh kuh-dah-sigh]

(At the) traffic light
shingou (de)   [shin-goh (deh)]

Go faster
Isoide kudasai   [ee-soh'ee-deh kuh-dah-sigh]

Slow down
Yukkuri itte kudasai   [it-teh kuh-dah-sigh]

Asking for Directions

Where is Shinjuku?
Shinjuku wa doko desuka   [shin-juh-kuh wah doh-koh dess-kah]

How do I get to Tokyo station?
Tokyo eki niwa douyatte ikimasuka
[toh-k'yoh eh-kee knee-wah doh-yat-teh ee-kee-mass-kah]

Example of a Simple Journey

Hello. Go to Shibuya, please.
Konnichiwa Shibuya ni itte kudasai

At the lights, turn right, then turn left.
Shingou de, migi ni magatte, sorekara, hidari ni magatte kudasai

Stop here. Thank you.
Koko de tomatte kudasai. Arigatou gozaimasu.

In a Restaurant

Getting a Table

People, 'persons'	*nin*	[nin]
How many people?	*Nanmei sama desuka*	[nan-may sah-mah dess-kah]
(1,2,3...) people:		
1 person	*hitori*	[h'toh-ree]
2 people	*futari*	[h'tah-ree]
3 people	*san-nin*	[san-nin]
4 people	*yo-nin*	[yoh-nin]
5 people	*go-nin*	[goh-nin]
6 people	*roku-nin*	[roh-kuh-nin]
7 people	*shichi-nin*	[sh'chee-nin]
8 people	*hachi-nin*	[hah-chee-nin]
9 people	*kyuu-nin*	[k'yuuh-nin]
10 people	*juu-nin*	[juuh-nin]

Food

Meat	*niku*	[knee-kuh]
Beef	*gyuuniku*	[g'yuuh-knee-kuh]
Chicken	*toriniku*	[toh-ree-knee-kuh]
Lamb	*ramu*	[rah-muh]
Pork	*butaniku*	[buh-tah-knee-kuh]
Fish	*sakana*	[sah-kah-nah]
Sushi	*sushi*	[suh-shee]
Vegetables	*yasai*	[yah-sigh]
Vegetarian dishes	*bejitarian ryouri*	

[beh-jee-tah-ree'an r'yoh-ree]

I'm a vegetarian *watashi wa bejitarian desu*
[wah-tah-shee wah beh-jee-tah-ree'an dess]

Rice	*gohan*	[goh-han]
Food	*tabemono*	[tah-beh-moh-noh]
Drink	*nomimono*	[noh-mee-moh-noh]
To eat	*tabemasu*	[tah-beh-mass]
To drink	*nomimasu*	[noh-mee-mass]

Ordering
There are various ways you can order in a restaurant, bar or coffee shop.

A. I will have... (*Watashi wa...ni shimasu*)
We can translate this to an English equivalent as "I will have...", although the Japanese verb 'to do' is used.

e.g. **I will have sushi**   *Watashi wa sushi ni shimasu*
[wah-tah-shee wah suh-shee knee shee-mass]

I'll have a coffee   *Watashi wa koohii ni shimasu*
[wah-tah-shee wah koh-hee knee shee-mass]

B. Please can I have..., please give me... (*...wo kudasai*)
'*Kudasai*' actually just means "...please", so state what it is you want, followed by '*...wo kudasai*'

Please give me soup
Soup wo kudasai   [soh'p kuh-dah-sigh]

Please give me 1 bowl of soup
Soup wo ippai kudasai   [soh'p woh ip-pie kuh-dah-sigh]

Please give me (1 / 2 / 3) ...
...wo (hitotsu / hutatsu / mittsu) kudasai
[woh (h'toh-ts'uh / h'tah-ts'uh / mit-ts'uh) kuh-dah-sigh]

C. Please bring me... (*...motte kite kudasai*)
'*Motte kuru*' means bring, so here, we say, "Item *wo* – number – bring – please"

e.g. **Please <u>bring</u> me 2 bottles of beer**
Biiru wo ni-hon <u>motte kite</u> kudasai
[bee-ruh woh knee-hon mot-teh kee-teh kuh-dah-sigh]

In the examples above, you can see the construction for ordering a number of bottles / glasses / plates / bowls etc of something. This is: **Item *wo* – number (select from the 2 lists over the page) – please.**
  e.g. **Gohan wo nihai kudasai** – 2 bowls of rice, please
  e.g. **Koora wa ippon kudasai** – 1 bottle of cola, please

When saying how many you would like of something in Japanese, different words are used for different items (for more on this, you can see the <u>Stating How Many</u> section in the Numbers chapter). For now, it will be enough just to see the words needed for food and drink containers in a restaurant.

Bai: bowls, plates, cups, glasses of food & drink

1	*ippai*	[ip-pie]
2	*nihai*	[knee-high]
3	*sanbai*	[san-bye]
4	*yonhai*	[yon-high]
5	*gohai*	[goh-high]
6	*roppai*	[rop-pie]
7	*nanahai*	[nah-nah-high]
8	*happai*	[hap-pie]
9	*kyuuhai*	[k'yuuh-high]
10	*juppai*	[juh'p-pie]

Hon/pon: bottles

1	*ippon*	[ip-pon]
2	*nihon*	[knee-hon]
3	*sanbon*	[san-bon]
4	*yonhon*	[yon-hon]
5	*gohon*	[goh-hon]
6	*roppon*	[rop-pon]
7	*nanahon*	[nah-nah-hon]
8	*happon*	[hap-pon]
9	*kuuhon*	[kuuh-hon]
10	*juppon*	[juh'p-pon]

Useful Language

Waiter   *ueita*   [uh-ay-tah]
(but to call the waiter: *"Sumimasen!"* [suh-mee-mah-sen])

Check / Bill   *O kanjou / o kaikei* [oh kan-joh / oh kye-kay]
(to request the check / bill: *"Sumimasen! O kaikei onegaishimasu."*)

Do you have...? *...wa arimasuka* [wah ah-ree-mass-kah]

Knife and fork *naihu to hooku* [nigh-huh toh hoh-kuh]
(Do you have a knife and fork? – *Naihu to fooku wa arimasuka*)

Chopsticks   *ohashi*   [oh-hah-shee]
(I can't use chopsticks – *Watashi wa ohashi wo tukaemasen*)

Spicy   *karai*   [kah-rye]
(Is this one spicy? – *Kore wa karai desuka*)
(I don't want it spicy – *Karakunaku shite kudasai*)

Menu   *menyuu*   [men-yuuh]
(Do you have an English menu? – *Eigo no menyuu wa arimasuka*)

Example of a simple visit

"Welcome. How many people?"
"Irassyaimase. Nanmei sama desuka"

4 people.
Yo-nin desu

...

Waiter!
Sumimasen

I'd like some tempura, please.
Tenpura wo kudasai

Please bring 4 bowls of rice.
Gohan wo yon-hai onegaishimasu

Do you have beer? Ok, please bring 4 bottles of beer.
Biiru wa arimasuka? Ok. Biiru wo yon-hon onegaishimasu.

Do you have a knife and fork?
Naihu to hooku wa arimasuka

Thank you very much.
Arigatou gozaimasu

...

Waiter! Check, please!
Sumimasen! O kaikei onegaishimasu!

Thank you very much.
Arigatou gozaimasu

In a Bar

Drinks

Alcoholic:

Beer	*biiru*	[bee-ruh]
White wine	*shirowain*	[shee-roh-wine]
Red wine	*akawain*	[ah-kah-wine]
Rice wine	*osake*	[oh-sah-keh]

Non-alcoholic:

Water	*mizu*	[mee-zuh]
Coke	*koora*	[koh-rah]
Sprite	*supuraito*	[s'puh-rye-toh]
Orange juice	*orenji-juusu*	[oh-ren-jee juuh-suh]
Coffee	*koohii*	[koh-hee]
Tea	*ocha*	[oh-chah]
Iced tea	*aisutei*	[eye-s'tay]

Ordering

Do you have...?	*...wa arimasuka*	[...wah ah-ree-mass-kah]
Do you have beer?	*Biiru wa arimasuka*	[bee-ruh wah ah-ree-mass-kah]

I will have...	*Watashi wa...*	[wah-tah-shee wah...]
I will have beer	*Watashi wa biiru*	[wah-tah-shee wah bee-ruh]

Please give me...   ...wo kudasai   [...woh kuh-dah-sigh]
Please give me 2 bottles of beer
Biiru wo ni-hon kudasai   [bee-ruh woh knee-hon kuh-dah-sigh]

Please bring another {1 / 2}
Mou (no.) onegaishimasu   [moh... oh-neh-guy-shee-mass]

Numbers (when ordering)

General

1	hitotsu	[h'toh-ts'uh]
2	hutatsu	[h'tah-ts'uh]
3	mittsu	[mit-ts'uh]
4	yottsu	[yot-ts'uh]
5	itsutsu	[ee-ts'uh-ts'uh]
6	muttsu	[muh't-ts'uh]
7	nanatsu	[nah-nah-ts'uh]
8	yattsu	[yat-ts'uh]
9	kokonotsu	[koh-koh-noh-ts'uh]
10	tou	[toh]

Bai: bowls, plates, cups, glasses of food & drink

1	ippai	[ip-pie]
2	nihai	[knee-high]
3	sanbai	[san-bye]
4	yonhai	[yon-high]
5	gohai	[goh-high]
6	roppai	[rop-pie]
7	nanahai	[nah-nah-high]
8	happai	[hap-pie]
9	kyuuhai	[k'yuuh-high]
10	juppai	[juh'p-pie]

Hon/pon: bottles

1	ippon	[ip-pon]
2	nihon	[knee-hon]
3	sanbon	[san-bon]
4	yonhon	[yon-hon]
5	gohon	[goh-hon]
6	roppon	[rop-pon]
7	nanahon	[nah-nah-hon]
8	happon	[hap-pon]
9	kuuhon	[kuuh-hon]
10	juppon	[juh'p-pon]

In a Shop

Price & Bargaining

How much (is this)?
(Kore wa) ikura desuka   [(koh-reh wah) ee-kuh-rah dess-kah]

How much (is that)?
(Sore wa) ikura desuka   [(soh-reh wah) ee-kuh-rah dess-kah]

1000 Yen
Sen-en desu   [sen-en dess]

It's too expensive
Takasugi masu   [tah-kah-suh-ghee mass]

Do you have anything cheaper?
Motto yasui mono wa arimasuka
[mot-toh yah-suh'ee moh-noh wah ah-ree-mass-kah]

Size & Colour

Do you have bigger?
Motto ookii mono wa arimasuka
[mot-toh oh-kee moh-noh wah ah-ree-mass-kah]

Do you have smaller?
Motto chiisai mono wa arimasuka
[mot-toh chee-sigh moh-noh wah ah-ree-mass-kah]

Do you have another colour?
Hoka no iro wa arimasuka
[hoh-kah noh ee-roh wah ah-ree-mass-kah]

Making Your Purchase

I'd like this ("This, please")
Kore wo kudasai   [koh-reh woh kuh-dah-sigh]

I don't want that
Sore wa irimasen   [soh-reh wah ee-ree-mah-sen]

I want the receipt ("Receipt, please")
Reshiito wo kudasai   [reh-shee-toh woh kuh-dah-sigh]

94

EXTRAS

15. Some Japanese Gestures & the Using the Term 'San'

'San'

First, and very briefly, the word 'san' in Japanese is used respectfully, and is similar to 'Mr.', 'Mrs.', 'Miss.' and 'Ms.' in English. It is stated after a person's name, and you will hear it used a lot more often than those closest terms in English. Use it with people you meet each time you say their name.

First name: *John-san*
Surname: *Tanaka-san*
Profession / title (Dr.): *Oisha-san*

Gestures

Japanese gestures are a little different to ours in the West. Here are just a few to aid you in the beginning, and you will be able to learn more when you are there.

Greeting People (Bowing)

As is well known almost anywhere you go, the Japanese form of greeting is bowing (not shaking hands etc). This is what you should do when you meet people, and here are a few general guidelines.

- The lower and longer you bow, the more respect you are showing. However, it is a good rule of thumb to bow to about 30 degrees, for no more than 2 seconds.

- Bend from the waist and keep your back straight.

- Your head should turn downwards with the bow too, and there should be no eye contact.

- Be natural – think about when we shake hands in the West too, and how it feels when someone is so stiff and uncomfortable that you can feel it in their handshake. Bowing is a normal means of greeting, and so is done naturally.

- Men: Keep your arms by your sides with the palms of your hands touching your legs. Lean forward and bow your head.

- Women: Keep your arms in front of your body, with hands joined, resting at the top of your legs. Lean forward and bow your head.

- Sometimes, you will also be offered a hand (which comes from Western hand-shaking) while you bow, in which case you should accept it, and continue bowing at the same time.

- Bowing continues each time you meet someone throughout the day, and not just when you meet for the first time that day.

Giving and Receiving Gifts or Business Cards

- To receive, extend both your arms, and take what you are given with both hands.

- To give, offer it in a like manner, holding it out with both hands.

Avoiding Pointing
To be polite, it is best to avoid pointing with your finger, and there are some ways this is done in Japan.

- To get someone's attention, raise one hand, open palm, towards the person. To get this right, put both hands in front of you as if you are praying, then put one hand down so just one is left up (to gain attention).

- To indicate (point to) someone, hold your hand open and palm-up, and point it in the direction of the person you wish to indicate.

16. A Summary of What You Will Need

This list is basically a reiterating of the table of contents but with slightly more detail. Have a look through this summary to see if there are any areas you don't feel confident, and revisit the relevant chapters if so.

- Sentences – Basic sentence word order (Subject/Topic + wa – Qu. Word – Indirect object + *ni* – Direct Object + wo – Extra info – Verb).

- Pronouns – *Watashi, anata, kara, kanojo, watashitachi, anatatachi, karera + wa, wo, ni, no, no mono.*

- Verbs – the 3 groups, some common verbs to use to get around, and their basic forms – Present/Future: *-masu, -masen;* Past: *-mashita, - masendeshita;* Question: *-ka;* Want to: *-tai desu;* Polite request: *-te kudasai;* Can: *-emasu/-emasen;* Must: *- bekidesu.*

- The Verb 'to be' – *desu, imasu & arimasu*
- *Desu* & its Forms – Present: *desu, dewa arimasen;* Past: *demashita, dewa arimasen deshita;* Question: *-ka.*

- Some common nouns & how to use them, including particles & plurals.

- Some common adjectives & how to use them, '*i*' adjectives and '*na*' adjectives & their endings.

- Questions & question words – *ka, nan/nani, dare, doko, itsu, doushite, donoyouni.*

- This, that, which, here, there & where – *kore, sore, are, dore; kono, sono, ano, dono; koko, soko, asoko, doko.*

- Other useful Phrases, including answering questions, making requests, modifying, distinguishing, time vocab, location

- Numbers, including counting, stating how many and how to tell the time.

- Basic Conversation – being able to ask and answer some basic questions

- Japanese phrases for various situations, including in a taxi, restaurant, bar and shop

17. Also Available & Final Note

Also Available

Please visit the Most Basic Languages website (**mostbasiclanguages.com**), where you will find the things outlined below (please note that if you are an early visitor, this is in the process of being expanded, and more is continually being added if you continue to check back). There is also a Facebook page, (**https://www.facebook.com/pages/Most-Basic-Languages/176905519122610**) where news of any free products will be posted.

Free Resources:
- I am trying to create and offer as many free resources as I can too. This will be notified via the Facebook page, and many resources will be available on Pinterest (**http://pinterest.com/jimmcg1/**), which I am just in the process of getting going, including language resources, top restaurants and bars, top travel tips and top schools (for those emigrating), among other things.

Phone Applications:
- At least one FREE app for every language covered. More are being designed and produced to be free.
- Other inexpensive apps designed to bring the easily accessible language of these books (The Most Basic _____).
- Further apps designed to enhance your language learning experience, including exercise books / apps to complement these books, as well as more apps to improve your travel experience.

Travel Apps & Books by Request:
If you have anything you would love to see in an app related to languages, travel or living abroad, or a specialized phrasebook of any kind, then simply send an email to **info@mostbasiclanguages.com,** and we will aim to have your app or book produced very quickly. It will then be made available cheaply for yourself and others to receive the benefits from.

*** This means that you can have any app or phrasebook you can think of to enhance your travel or language learning experience, within a short time of requesting it. ***

Other books:

- The Most Basic Language Series
All the basics needed to get by in a country, when travelling or living there. This series is being rapidly expanded to include more languages. The books included so far in this series are:

- The Most Basic Chinese – All You Need to Know to Get By
- The Most Basic Japanese – All You Need to Know to Get By
- The Most Basic Lithuanian – All You Need to Know to Get By
- The Most Basic Vietnamese – All You Need to Know to Get By

- The Most Vital Language Series

This is a series of short e-booklets, outlining days, dates and the vocabulary needed for staying in a hotel, and which I try to make **free** to download on Amazon on the 1st and 15th of each month. The books included so far in this series are:
- The Most Vital Chinese
- The Most Vital Vietnamese

More to come:

- More "**The Most Basic ___**" language books and apps to come. I am currently working with people on a number of other languages to expand the series, as well as converting the series into Android and IOS Applications which will also include the ability to listen to the pronunciation of a native speaker. Please keep an eye out for these in the near future if you are interested.

Final Note

To us in the West, Japan is an exciting place, full of mystique, with its ancient culture and rich history. We have all seen movies and heard stories of the honour-based culture, and Japanese customs such as bowing, clothes such as the kimono, and activities like sumo wrestling are famous the world over.

However, most Westerners have little direct experience of Japan and Japanese people, which is a shame, and if you get a chance to meet and converse with some of the locals, you will enjoy your trip so much more. Speaking with real people (in any country) is far different to watching stereotypes portrayed through the media, and you will meet some truly fascinating people if you wish to.

So if you have any desire or plans to travel or work in Japan, then make the effort to learn the basic language presented in this booklet book, and your experience will be greatly enhanced. Also, just like in a lot of other countries, many locals do not speak English, and you will be appreciated for trying to speak to them in their own language.

Good luck, learn the language in the book and make the most of your trip!